# Stop, Drop & Deal

## Your Suffering Has Significance

# Vicki O'Brien

Vicki O'Brien
Stop, Drop & Deal: Your Suffering Has Significance

Relevant Entertainment Press
Copyright ©2025 by Vicki O'Brien
First Edition

Softcover ISBN 979-8-9998086-0-8
eBook ISBN 979-8-9998086-1-5

For those who have experienced a deep, personal loss of some kind or who are walking through a time of tremendous pain and don't know how or when it will end, this book is for you. If you find yourself unable to breathe or having to literally force yourself to take the next step in order to keep going, this book is for you. If you feel lost, confused, scared, and unsure of what life holds, or just have no idea how to escape "the debilitating stupor" that has gripped your heart and life, this book is for you. If you feel as if you are only seen through the lens of your circumstances instead of being seen and understood for who you are, this book is for you too.

Above all, this book is my heartfelt attempt to acknowledge the relationship I have with the Lord. My connection with God made it possible to have my sweet and intimate relationship— of more than twenty years—with my husband Dave, but more importantly, it has and continues to give me life.

# Contents

Introduction . . . . . . . . . . . . . . . . . . . . . . . . . . . . . . . . . . . . . . . . . . . . 9

**Chapter One:** Words Matter . . . . . . . . . . . . . . . . . . . . . . . . . . . . . . . 15

**Chapter Two:** Relationships Are Difficult ... Period!. . . . . . . . . . . . . 19

**Chapter Three:** Perseverance Born from Adversity Transforms Us. . . 29

**Chapter Four:** God's Methods Are Often Unexpected . . . . . . . . . . . 41

**Chapter Five:** Comfort Is the Enemy of Growth . . . . . . . . . . . . . . . . . 53

**Chapter Six:** Your Choices Determine Your Experience . . . . . . . . . . 65

**Chapter Seven:** Letting Go Is Necessary . . . . . . . . . . . . . . . . . . . . . . . 91

**Chapter Eight:** Grief Is a Funny Thing . . . . . . . . . . . . . . . . . . . . . . . . 105

**Conclusion:** Trust the Master Painter. . . . . . . . . . . . . . . . . . . . . . . . . 123

**Epilogue:** A Letter to Young Widows. . . . . . . . . . . . . . . . . . . . . . . . . 131

**Acknowledgments.** . . . . . . . . . . . . . . . . . . . . . . . . . . . . . . . . . . . . . . 141

# Introduction

Familiar and comfortable professionally, yet foreign and undesirable personally, the moment about to take place would bring me face-to-face with a heartbreaking finality and mark the beginning of the next step on this inconceivable journey. As our friend Brad finished his opening remarks and introduced me, I stood up and took what felt like the longest and most difficult steps of my life to the stairs of the stage as I walked up and stood behind the podium. Feeling the uncomfortable silence and heartache in the room while looking into row upon row of familiar faces, I was flooded with conflicting emotions and thoughts. Although my heart was focused on honoring Dave and our life together, all that was running through my mind was how fervently I desired to wake up from this nightmare as the feelings of numbness, brokenness, emptiness, shock, isolation, intense sadness, and frustration from the never-ending looks of pity consumed me. So, I took a breath, asked the Lord for supernatural strength, and reminded myself that today was for Dave. Then, I began to speak the first words of Dave's eulogy.

On December 15, 2023, at the young age of forty-eight, my husband Dave went home to be with the Lord. This caught me and everyone in our lives completely off guard, as Dave had never been seriously ill a day in his adult life, not to mention the fact that we both worked hard to be fit and health conscious in all of our lifestyle choices. So, the question for many people became "How did this happen?" The truth of the matter is layered and deep, and a good part of it will never be known this side of eternity.

If I'm being completely transparent and honest, I had no intention or desire to write a book about my personal journey through this season of my life. As someone who has always believed in the sanctity of personal relationships and protecting them at all costs, I wanted to keep doing just that. However, as the one-year mark since Dave's passing recently took place, I found myself neck-deep in the quicksand of my current reality, and I was sidelined by the fact that I literally had nothing more to give—mentally, physically, emotionally, or spiritually—to anyone or anything else. All I could do was sit down and wait on the Lord to come meet me because I was spent and exhausted. I was done. I had to *stop*.

It was during this two-week time span that the Lord ministered to me in some specific and much-needed ways, as well as convicted me of something. He gently reminded me that as humans, we are not capable of giving something we haven't received ourselves, nor are we capable of truly understanding something we have never experienced ourselves. Although this is not the sole reason for everything that has happened in my life over the past few years, I now know that one of the reasons for this season of struggle was so I could empathize and walk hand-in-hand with others who have experienced loss and are going through a season of grief, which is one of the most intimate and loving things we can do with another human being.

Life is fragile, short, and unpredictable, to say the least. Whether we like it or not, and whether we choose it or not, pain and loss are features of this life. And because, as we just discussed, personal experience is the best teacher of empathy, pain and loss become a necessary element of life for anyone wanting to authentically connect with others. I didn't say it was desirable or fun, but nevertheless, it is necessary. So, the question then becomes, "How do we navigate this necessary menace when it comes our way in a manner that remains connected to truth, authentic to who we are, and doesn't completely destroy us in the process?" Because the ugly truth is that deep-seated pain and loss tend to uproot even the most grounded of hearts, which, in turn, leaves a trail of destruction that is littered with feelings of loneliness, fear, emptiness, isolation, worthlessness, guilt, anger, resentment, confusion, and so much more. All of which I have experienced at one time or another on this unexpected journey.

To add insult to injury, I never fully understood the largely ignored reality of loss for young widows until now. Although death and loss are painful and hard to accept at any age, experiencing them at a young age brings a unique set of what can feel like "insurmountable" obstacles into your life, whose only purpose seems to be adding more heartache, pain, and a sense of hopelessness to the pain and desperation that already exists. Learning to accept and navigate these times can be a lonely and difficult road in and of itself, but discovering that there really are no established societal support solutions for those who find themselves on this road of life at an unexpected age makes it feel even more impossible to navigate.

My hope and prayer in sharing my story with you is two-fold. First, I hope that it will not only bring comfort, encouragement, and optimism for a brighter future, but also remind you that you are not alone. Man was not created to walk this life alone. We learn this in the first few chapters of the first book of the Bible, in Genesis 2:18: "And the Lord God said, 'It is not good that man should be alone; I will make him a helper comparable to him.'" Now, yes, this verse is a reference to the creation of Eve for Adam. However, the concept of humans needing companions with which to walk this life goes beyond the relationship of husband and wife. As humans, we are created to experience and "do" life with other humans in an intimate way. But, we are also created for an even more intimate and fulfilling relationship with our Creator. So, why is it that when life gets hard, messy, or just flat-out starts spinning out of control, more often than not (at least, this is true for me), we shrink inward and don't want other people to know what we are experiencing, and therefore, try to go it alone? Although there are multiple reasons that lead people to choose this path, it never works because it opposes how we were created to function. This means that until we are willing to get comfortable with the uncomfortable, we will never be able to break through and experience life to the fullest, as God intends for each of us. Second, my heart's cry for everyone reading this book is that you are able to come to the place of understanding that your suffering is not without significance. After all, pain without purpose is just pain, which is meaningless. I choose to believe that our lives have meaning. So, although what you are experiencing or have experienced may feel random and uninvited, part of the healing journey requires discovering the purpose behind the suffering, which is quite often obscured in the midst of the sea of pain. Therefore, it requires the process of discovery to uncover it.

There is another important element of this book and my journey that I would like to mention. Like you and everyone else, I can only speak from the vantage point of my personal experiences and beliefs, which may differ from yours. My Christian beliefs and relationship with the Lord play an integral role in every area of my life, and they have significantly shaped my journey of tremendous loss and pain. However, I'd like to point out that pain and loss are languages that need no translation, as they are universal and can bring humans together to build each other up despite other differences. Therefore, I encourage you to approach this story with that unifying perspective. Although this book is not intended to target your personally held beliefs, the process of peeling back the layers of the onion as we discuss what is at the heart of the brokenness that people are experiencing naturally leads to some of our personal beliefs being challenged. At least this was and is true for me. Why? Because this is part of any healthy discovery, change, and healing process. Please notice that I said "being challenged" and not "being changed." What you do with the information is completely up to you. My goal is to merely offer up the missing pieces of the puzzle I uncovered along this journey based on facts, my experiences, and my belief system. It is up to you how or if you implement what is shared. Therefore, my encouragement to you is to be willing to come face-to-face with some hard truths (like I have had to do), and as a result, be willing to sit, feel, and deal with your situation. True transformation always requires change, and change always begins with the revelation and acceptance of truth.

When I first considered what to write, I was unsure how to accurately express my current reality and detail everything I have learned on this journey. I was repeatedly drawn back to the eulogy that I gave at my husband's funeral. Although I didn't understand why at first, as I read through it a few times more, the reason became clear. The deeper reasons and meaning behind everything I had experienced and was still currently battling could all be found within the eulogy itself. I felt like I was given another chance to voice the unspoken words and concepts that were held within.

So, that's why we started this introduction with the final moments before I got up on stage to deliver the eulogy. The first seven chapters begin with a portion of the eulogy and the last chapter expands on the unspoken concept conveyed within those words. It is my sincere hope and prayer for everyone who reads this that you will be willing to open the door of your heart and allow the light of honesty to expose your pain, loss, and suffering in a raw and vulnerable way. In spite of how painful it might be, choose to stop and feel whatever it is that needs to surface so that you give your pain a voice, which is the only way we are able to begin to truly deal with what is going on inside and navigate through the process in a way that makes it possible for true and complete healing to take place.

# CHAPTER ONE

# Words Matter

I have always believed and said that words matter ... because they do. Dave would constantly say to me "You're the word magician!" That was typically in response to something like the word *simply*, to which I would reply, "It's not magic, Dave, it's called *phonics!*" That's the result of a life that relies on spellcheck, friends! Dave was super sharp and one of the most intelligent people I have ever known; he just couldn't spell and often was at odds with grammar. I jokingly said to him all the time, "You can use the word if you can spell it." I'm sure you can imagine the look and response that got me ...

In all seriousness, our words matter because Jesus is the living Word. John 1:1 tells us, "In the beginning was the Word, and the Word was with God, and the Word was God." And for those of us who claim the name of Jesus Christ, this living Word resides in us. Therefore, the words that come out of our mouths, as well as what our lives speak through the way we live, matter.

One of my favorite sayings comes from something I heard repeatedly growing up, and that is

"Relationship is the most important word in the English language." This has always resonated with me so deeply because relationships are at the center of everything in our existence, physically and spiritually. As a matter of fact, all of you are here today because of a relationship you have with me, with Dave, or with both of us. And I am here today because of two amazing relationships that the Lord has afforded me in this life. You see, my relationship with the Lord has allowed me to have this sweet and intimate relationship with Dave for more than twenty years.

These were the opening words for the most important and absolutely most difficult talk of my life to date: my husband's eulogy. Although I had zero desire to speak in any capacity at Dave's funeral, I was strongly convicted to do so, as no one else could speak to our lives in a way that would suffice. Deep down, I knew that I owed it to Dave, our marriage, everyone who attended his funeral, and the Lord to speak freely and openly about our relationship, struggles, life, and the present reality in which I found myself.

It was during the preparation process for this chapter that I began thoughtfully pondering the importance of our words. So, what exactly is it about words that allow them to shape and even alter the course of our lives? Simply put, words have power. But what makes them unique is that words wield power in a way that nothing else can. This is not a new or foreign concept to most of us. However, do you know from where this truth originates? It literally comes from the Word of God. "A man's stomach shall be satisfied from the fruit of his mouth; From the produce of his lips he shall be filled. Death and life are in the power of the tongue, And those who love it will eat its fruit" (Proverbs 18:20–21). The very power of life and death itself are held within the power of our words—a truth that has more ramifications in this life than most of us can even begin to comprehend. This is especially true when it comes to dealing with pain and suffering that can so easily overtake our hearts, minds, and lives. Therefore, being able to speak words of truth in any and all circumstances to others and ourselves is not only a revelator of the heart, but also a critical piece to the healing process.

Words are also a way to give the unspoken feelings, thoughts, and state of your soul a voice with which to release the pressure threatening not only to rupture your soul, but your entire being. The act of speaking honestly towards and about anything in life is the first step of courage required on the path of healing and restoration. Because whether we say them out loud or merely speak them quietly to ourselves within the shelter of our minds, the reality is that we are either speaking death or life over ourselves and/or others with these words. Therefore, being able to rightly delineate the words that we are speaking to others, as well as to ourselves, helps us get closer to revealing the true heart of the matter.

With that being said, maybe now you better understand why I believe *relationship* is the most important word in the English language. As humans, we are created to connect and relate to the world around us. We do this by establishing connections. Establishing relationships requires connection. A significant portion of being able to connect with another human being is centered on communication, which encompasses words. Therefore, words matter, especially in the context of relationships. The trajectory and outcome of relationships often hinges on the words that are spoken and—more often than we choose to admit—the words left unspoken. Just like words, relationships wield power. Both are important instruments that when operated appropriately give the encouragement and strength that is needed to just keep going. So, I invite you to take a walk with me.

# CHAPTER TWO

# Relationships Are Difficult ... Period!

As we all know, relationships are full of ups and downs, good and bad, heartache and joy, laughter and tears, struggle and victory. Mine and Dave's was no different. As a matter of fact, the first seven or eight years of our marriage embodied the roller coaster ride that is learning how "the two shall become one flesh." Easy to say, but harder to do. I have often been heard saying that this marriage taught me the true meaning of the phrase "Till death do us part" because there were times when we were both thinking, "Lord, I don't believe in divorce or walking away, so the question is who is going to die at whose hands first?" If you've been married for any length of time, you know exactly what I mean.

In the early days, our biggest fights came in fast-food drive-thru lines. Ridiculous ... I know! I realize this is hard for many who know me to believe because I am so health conscious and eat as clean and natural as possible, but keep in mind, we got married in college. We were a couple of broke college kids with strong immune systems, and apparently steel stomachs considering everything we ate back then! To my embarrassment now, many a time, I could be seen getting out of the car in a drive-thru line and walking away while, let's just say, I was voicing my opinion rather loudly—all to the amusement of other cars and people standing nearby. Now, before you write me off as a crazy Texas girl (okay, I admit that I've got a little hitch in my giddy up), I had my reasons. It was always due to the fact that Dave didn't want to give the person taking the order my changes to the food because, and I quote, "It would make their job harder." Seriously!?

You see, Dave was an easygoing guy in most areas, and he would eat almost anything you put before him. He never wanted to inconvenience anyone. In these early years, we found ourselves in the Burger King drive-thru quite often. The thought of that today makes me regurgitate in my mouth a little, but hey, it was cheap and they were everywhere! (No offense intended to those of you who like Burger King.) My response to Dave not wanting to give my requests to the person taking the order was usually something along the lines of, "Are you kidding me? Their motto is Have it your way! That's Bon Qui Qui's job. Just stinking tell them 'no mayonnaise and no onions' already!"

Then, there were the disagreements about how to properly wash clothes and load the dishwasher.

For some reason still unbeknownst to me, the world would come to an end if I washed towels with his boxers. Not because I mixed colors with whites or because I would bleach and ruin the look of his boxers. You want to know why this was a cardinal sin in Dave's book? He said it's because washing towels with his boxers would leave lint balls on the rim of the boxers! Isn't that why lint rollers were invented? Anyway, he decided the solution for me "not knowing how to do laundry properly" was to handle the laundry himself. If that's my punishment, then punish me all day! Right? That's how you do it, ladies. Just kidding.

All of this to say, our marriage and relationship was not perfect—far from it. The struggles were real. But it was a beautiful work in which the Lord was carving out his image more clearly in each of us, which is exactly what the Lord designed marriage to be, if we will allow it. Marriage was always meant to represent to the world the holy covenant and union we were created to have with the Lord. Therefore, how we walk it out in this world matters, and the truth is, our marriages are a reflection of the level of intimacy and connection we either have or don't with the Lord, as well as an understanding of ourselves at an intimate level.

I have always believed that the foundation for any strong and lasting dating or marriage relationship is a solid friendship. Why is this? Once again, I believe it's because we were created to connect to the world and people around us, and we do this by establishing relationships. As we discussed in chapter 1, the first aspect of any relationship is a connection: something that draws the two parties together, which is usually a shared interest. As all of us know, it's not a requirement to have everything, or even most things, in common in order to be friends with someone. However, the best friendships in our lives are those with whom we share more commonalities and interests than not, especially when it comes to the important things in life. These are the relationships that we choose to nourish consistently and deeply, and these are the people with whom we desire to walk life daily. Otherwise known as *our people.*

Dave was my best friend. We both had a deep desire to marry someone that we not only liked as a person, but also with whom we shared mutual hobbies, passions, and outlooks on life itself, and we found that to be very true in our relationship. We had things in common where it mattered most, yet, we were very different in ways that complemented the other perfectly. He was strong in areas where I was weak and he challenged me in ways I needed, which allowed the two pieces of the puzzle to fit together and complement one another nicely.

However, believe it or not, it was not love at first sight for me. Call me clueless (as Dave always did when it came to picking up on clues from the opposite sex), but it took me a hot minute before I realized Dave was interested in dating me, and an even longer time for me to consider the prospect of a relationship. Although there's a little more to the story of why this was the case, I was that girl who had more guy friends than girl friends most of her life. This was, in large part, because not only was I a daddy's girl, but I had played competitive sports since the age of five (I know this sounds young, but my dad was a professional baseball player when he was young, which meant I had a glove in my hand before I could throw). So, let's just say that my mentality and methods of dealing with things in life leaned more towards the "suck it up, buttercup, because life isn't easy" mindset versus the typical, more emotionally driven response of the average girl. Not saying that one is better than the other; just stating the reality of who I am for better or worse.

Because of this, I have always been drawn to friendships with people who are not prone to emotional swings and being constantly stressed, which more often than not, meant friendships with guys. I did have a few good girl friends growing up and still do today, just not as many as guys. Life and personal maturity in the area of accepting differences in others has balanced that out over the years.

Another big reason I had more guy friends is that I was the only girl amongst all the boys my age at church, beginning from around the third grade and right through to high school graduation. As a matter of fact, the picture from my high school baccalaureate is of me and the five guys from church who had been my closest friends since kindergarten. What's odd to me, and still surprises me, is that most people who hear this fact find it hard to believe that I never dated any of those guys. Now, don't get me wrong, that doesn't mean that I didn't have a fleeting teenage infatuation with one or two of them at some point (and no ... I will never divulge which ones they were. Some things are only for a girl to know), but my relationship and love for each of them ran deeper than any mere infatuation, and that fact allowed me to have a meaningful and intimate relationship with them. As a matter of fact, my best guy friend growing up from this group, Scott McDonald, was my date to prom, which made the experience so much more fun and relaxing than if I had gone with a boyfriend. Having this type of relationship with the opposite sex was something that I needed to experience more than I could have ever known, not only for those years in my life, but also for what my future would hold.

You see, I am the youngest of two kids. My older brother, Tim, is almost four years older than me and was born with cerebral palsy. This affected the entire right side of his body. He operated at the equivalent of a nine year old mentally all of his life, as well as walked with a limp and had stunted use of his right hand. This meant that I had to look out for my older brother, even though he was always trying to do the same for me in the best way he knew. Even though Tim had these physical and mental challenges and limitations, make no mistake, the boy knew how to push my buttons to get his way—and he did so quite often! In this way, we had a typical sibling relationship. I love my brother more than words can or will ever express, and I know he felt the same about me. Watching Tim live his life to the fullest in spite of his extremely challenging days taught me invaluable lessons about what is really important in life. However, the reality of his situation forced me to accept that I'd never have the brother-sister relationship that I had desired.

As I mentioned earlier, I have always been a proud daddy's girl. So, I was naturally drawn to my dad, and the connection was mutual. My dad loved my brother, and it was hard for him to see his only son with severe physical and mental limitations and not be able to do anything about it or share his life passions with him. So, I became the closest and next best outlet for him. My dad never pushed anything on me; he didn't have to do that. I loved many things that he loved, and this was largely due to our similar personalities. You could say that my dad was the person who knew me best, a.k.a. my best friend when I was young. Once a week when I was in elementary school, he would take me to Jack in the Box before school for breakfast (I loved their Breakfast Jacks) as a daddy-daughter date. The strange thing is that I don't remember us ever really having meaningful conversations during these times; instead, we would just sit in one another's company and eat. My dad, as was his routine, would work on the daily crossword puzzle and drink coffee while I ate. Even though I am a communicator by nature (my mom said that I didn't need to be spanked or encouraged to try and make noise as I came out of the womb crying!) and would have loved to talk with him, I knew that wasn't his nature. So, it didn't bother me to sit in silence with him, as I knew that quality time with me was his way of showing me he loved me. We share this love language. I wholeheartedly believe this also taught me how to cherish just being in the moment with someone without words. Our presence and expressions can sometimes convey more than words ever could.

When I say that I was devastated and felt as if a part of me had been ripped out and killed when my dad suddenly passed, it should come as no surprise. I was only thirteen when this happened. My entire world was upended, not only because I lost my best friend and father, but also because my mom went into a deep depression from which she never fully recovered, which in essence, left me to fend for myself emotionally, mentally, and in some ways physically. This included taking care of my brother to a large degree. I will go into more detail about the complicated relationship with my mom later, but I am sharing all of this background to say that I understand and can relate to messy and complicated family dynamics.

Contrary to what most people who meet me today think, I did not grow up with anything close to the "aspirational" family life or upbringing. As a matter of fact, when you learn about all of the things in my past, you see that I made the perfect poster child for the kid most likely to end up pregnant, in jail, or as a total menace to society. However, thanks to the grace of God and His work in my life, I was able to choose a different path, even if I couldn't answer the question "God, why can't I have a loving family like other people?"

Maybe some of you reading this can relate to "the hot mess express" of family relationships like mine. On the other hand, maybe my experience doesn't resonate with you because you have a great family support system; if that's the case, I'm thankful for you! However, even in the best ones, relationships are difficult to traverse at times because we live in a broken world, and unfortunately, at times, the struggles and mess we face isn't our own choosing.

An imperfect world means imperfect people who make mistakes, which leads to imperfect relationships. This was true even for Dave and me. Two different family situations being merged into a union can make a marriage relationship challenging, as well as two different personalities and general life experiences. Not to mention the "personal baggage" from the trauma and drama of life that most of us bring to this union. Dave and I experienced this firsthand. I wasn't the only one with a challenging family situation who had always dreamed she would marry into a family like the one she always wanted. The same was true for Dave. His family situation was nothing like mine, but it brought a wholly different set of challenges to the scene that Dave sought to escape. If I'm being totally honest here, a part of me thought I would never find someone to marry me because of my hot mess of a mom and lack of a functional family unit. Maybe subconsciously that is why I have always been so oblivious to the interest of the opposite sex. It's hard for me to believe that anyone would choose to take on such a situation, and I would never want that for another person, especially someone I loved. While in contrast, friends tend to accept all of who you are. So, finding Dave was an amazing reminder to me from the Lord that our circumstances don't define who we are unless we let them, and family is what we make it.

None of us get to choose the family into which we are born, but we each get to choose who we add to our family in this life (whether it be through marriage or friendships). Because of this, Dave and I became each other's family, and we were committed to creating a new family together that would be different, strong, and reflect what we believed a family should be. Relationships are hard because life is hard, and it is only when we learn to truly embrace this concept that we are able to work through the pain, struggle, and challenges of this life.

The most important unifying factor that existed between Dave and I was our mutual love for the Lord. However, as I said in the eulogy, the struggles were real in our relationship, which included the significant difference between our spiritual lives as well. As is often the case with couples, we both knew and had a relationship with the Lord, but we were at different places in that relationship. This difference brought unique challenges into our relationship that tested our resolve and will to persevere. In hindsight, I can say that understanding myself from God's perspective was vital to correctly understanding my role in every relationship, but especially my marriage. Until we know who we truly are, we will struggle to rightly connect with anyone else in any meaningful and intimate way, especially our significant other. Therefore, it will always require patient endurance on the part of both parties in order to see the end result of this beautiful masterpiece that the Lord is painting of the two becoming one.

# CHAPTER THREE

# Perseverance Born from Adversity Transforms Us

Dave was a quiet, grounded, multi-talented, no nonsense, loving, caring, and giving person whose personality had the ability to relate well with people from all walks of life, while at the same time, naturally bringing people together (this was true with family and friends alike). Although he would chat up those with whom he had good friendships, this wasn't true with other people. Dave was one of the most observant and discerning people I've ever known, especially when it came to accurately reading others immediately. If he didn't feel as if he had something in common or was able to intellectually or spiritually relate to someone else who was trying to converse with him, he would remain silent. This didn't come from a place of feeling superior or even judgement towards the other person, but instead, it came from the belief that his time and energy was too valuable to waste feigning interest, as well as he wanted to avoid saying something that might unintentionally hurt the other person. In this, he showed immense maturity and care for the well-being of others. A trait I admired, as it brought balance and a much-needed perspective to my chatty nature.

He was a jack-of-all-trades and a master of many. There wasn't too much that Dave didn't know how to do or fix, and he had multiple interests in vastly different areas. He was just as comfortable in a cowboy hat and boots as he was his leather riding jacket and motorcycle helmet. Whether it was for his help with fixing a vehicle or motorcycle, working on a boat, or building something from scratch (from a greenhouse to a chicken coop); being the general contractor on a home project; or discussing his passion for overlanding and video editing, Dave became the go-to person for many people in our sphere of influence. His natural intelligence, curiosity, willingness to work hard, desire to be the best at everything he did, and love of serving others caused his name and number to be on many people's repair/help list, and he loved it!

Everyone who met and knew Dave loved him and saw him as special. However, Dave struggled to see himself that way. Dave was raised in a household and family where the Bible was taught as truth and revered. Therefore, he believed God was who He said He was and that His Word (the Bible) was absolute truth. However, he always struggled internally with who he authentically was as a person and what it looks like to have an intimate walk with the Lord that is more than just "religious activities" such as going to church, reading the Bible, and "doing good things." He desired not only to have a relationship with the Lord where you know His voice when He speaks, and you don't doubt it when you hear it because you know it that well, but also to fully and intimately understand who he was created to be as a person. The way the Bible says Moses knew the Lord in Exodus 33:11 is incredible, "And the Lord spoke with Moses face to face, as a man speaks to a friend." Who wouldn't want this with the creator of the universe, who knows every single detail about us and this world? Dave wanted that type of intimacy.

Intellectually, he knew there was a difference between entering into a relationship with the Lord via a one-time prayer of salvation versus intimately knowing the Lord via a deep and meaningful relationship. But he didn't know how to bridge the gap. Dave would see this type of relationship in a person's life and desire that same level of intimacy and want to know how to get there himself, but it always seemed to elude him—as if it was for others to have and not for him. He expressed to me early on in our marriage that part of the reason for this was because he never really saw an example of this walked out from those closest to him in his reality, including his family. What he came to realize in the last few years of his life was that he had been leaning into his intellect to try and understand and relate to the Lord instead of allowing the Lord to bring the spirit inside of him to life by transforming his heart.

You see, friends, the truth is we are spirit beings wrapped in flesh, but most of us choose to walk in this flesh and try to relate to God, ourselves, this world, and others via fleshly ways (feelings, thoughts, inclinations, and our untransformed hearts) versus learning to worship Him in spirit and in truth, like the Word tells us we must. This can and only does happen when a transformation occurs in us. It's only when such a transformation takes place in our hearts that we can truly know God for who He is, and in turn, be intimately connected to who we were created to be. As Paul tells us in Romans 12:1–2, "I beseech you therefore, brethren, by the mercies of God, that you present your bodies a living sacrifice, holy, acceptable to God, which is your reasonable service. And do not be conformed to this world, but be transformed by the renewing of your mind, that you may prove what is that good and acceptable and perfect will of God." Dave came to realize that he needed to be transformed in order for this to happen, but he (like many of you, perhaps) struggled with trying to understand what this looks like in the real world, and how it happens. Why did this seem so easy for others and yet impossible for him? It frustrated and plagued him most of our marriage. For years, my prayer was that the Lord would draw Dave's heart to Him, and that He would create a hunger and thirst for His presence and His Word in Dave, and that He would do whatever it took to finish what He began in Dave.

As humans, we tend to think that the things and experiences that ultimately work out for our good should not bring pain or difficulty. However, I was reminded by these words that this couldn't be further from the truth.

I unequivocally believe there is a creator who loves us more than we can comprehend and longs for us to just walk with Him. By this, I mean consciously choosing to use our time and energy to get to know who He is, what He loves, what He hates, how He thinks, what He desires, how He views us, and then be willing to share all of these things about us with Him. Just as we would do with someone in an intimate partnership in this life. That's it! As humans, we want to make it so much more complicated than that, most likely because almost everything in this life is unnecessarily complicated. So, why do we so often choose the complicated path? I believe it's because this level of intimacy requires suffering and death to self. As anyone who has been in any type of long-term relationship knows, the success and longevity of that relationship hinges on being able to place the other person's needs ahead of your own. Otherwise known as death to self, which is usually undesirable and painful for us. Suffering and death to self are two things that run contrary to our human nature, and require complete vulnerability and trust on our part. In essence, it requires death to our unhealthy and selfish ways while trusting that the other person only has our best interests in mind, which is terrifying. I find this to be true for most people, including myself.

I don't know about you, but I absolutely despise all *religion* in every sense of the word. It's because religion (no matter what form it takes) runs in direct opposition to a relationship, which as we have discussed, is all the Lord wants from us. You see, it's not complicated, but rather harder than hell for us because it runs contrary to what our senses and the world around us tell us to do. This can only be understood when we are able to comprehend two important concepts.

First, the distinction between the meaning of the words *hard* and *complicated*. *Hard* means it requires considerable physical or mental effort, or, in other words, is challenging, demanding, and grueling. However, *complicated* is something that has many parts or aspects that are interrelated, or, in other words, is complex, compound, and difficult. Therefore, something that is simple in its nature (uncomplicated), often times, is hard to do. By contrast, something that is complicated is never simple and often impossible to do.

Second, that we are multi-dimensional creatures whose needs and desires are in a perpetual state of conflict with one another. Otherwise commonly referred to as *our internal struggle*. This is a battle between what our bodies communicate to us versus what our souls (conscience given to each of us by our Creator that innately knows right from wrong) speak to us. It is how we respond to our conscience that drives and determines the state of our bodies and spirits. Let me give you an easy-to-understand example of how this concept plays out in our everyday lives.

Choosing to either eat a bowl of fresh fruit or donuts for breakfast is a pretty straightforward (uncomplicated) choice when viewed merely through the lens of what's best for our overall health, right? However, when you add physical desires and cravings which cause your body to scream to you, "Go for the sugar-coated, frosted baked goods of pure joy for your mouth, stupid!" the choice now becomes hard. This is because what your body craves/desires and therefore speaks to your mind is not in alignment with what your conscience is speaking to your mind about what's best for your overall health. They are at odds with one another. Now, a simple choice has been made hard. You will continue to desire the donuts until you actively choose to bring your body and mind into alignment with your conscience by choosing to eat the fruit, in spite of your craving. When done repeatedly over time, guess what happens? Science has shown that your taste buds change, which in turn, changes your desires and cravings for healthy sugar (fruit) instead of the processed sugar (donuts). As a result, the mind and body are brought into alignment with one another.

Similar to our relationship with food, as humans, we tend to complicate our relationship with God, which is designed to be straightforward (uncomplicated), due to our fleshly (human) desires that run in opposition to what is best for our spirit. The path of religion merely exists to create an impediment to actually having a relationship with our Creator, which is what entangled Dave most of his life. Like Dave, I find that many people struggle with the concept of having an intimate relationship with the Lord. So, it's no wonder that we struggle with intimacy in other relationships such as marriages and friendships. How can we connect and pour into another person when we are disconnected with who we are at our most intimate level: our conscience and spirit? Even though my journey in developing an intimate relationship with the Lord may not look the same as Dave's, it has and still is not without struggle, heartache, and pain. It has been and continues to be difficult to maintain. This is true for all of us, friends.

An even deeper truth to consider is that struggle, pain, and heartache in life and relationships is a reality for all of us, whether you choose to believe and trust in God or not. This is the case due to what the Bible teaches, and the world itself clearly displays: that we are all created to be in relationship with God and with others, but sin has brought brokenness into the world. Now, how this specifically plays out for each of us may look different in the physical, but the design and intent is universal. Because of this, as humans, we all share an extremely strong need to be intimately known and understood by others. Unless we truly understand who we are and why we are here at an intimate level, how can we ever connect with or understand others in any significant way? The truth is we can't. We must face ourselves honestly, in order to honestly love, understand, and connect with others. Just like me, Dave said a prayer for salvation with the knowledge and belief that he needed to know the God of the universe in order to be made clean and right at the age of eight. But, there is a big difference between understanding the need and giving a portion of yourself versus giving all of yourself to God.

In a marriage relationship, until and unless we are able to give all of ourselves to the other person (this means willingly sharing all of your passions, loves, fears, hopes, dreams, insecurities, challenges, beauty, and ugliness), we will never be able to experience true intimacy, peace, love, and acceptance within that marriage. I believe the same is true with the Lord. This can and does only happen when we truly believe that the other person has our best interests in mind and loves us as we are. When we can believe this, we can begin to walk down the path of understanding, or at the very least, accept the need for struggle and heartache in this life. That doesn't mean we have to like it; that would be crazy! But it does mean that we are able to view it as a tool to help deepen our connection with others and with the Lord instead of merely as an instrument of destruction and as a source of needless pain in our lives.

It's a funny concept that pain and destruction are used to bring strength and healing, but we need look no further than the human body to see this. (I will do my best to not "nerd out too much" on you here, but this type of example comes all too natural to someone with a degree in biology.) The physical process of building muscle in the human body is destructive and painful. Do you realize that in order to build new muscle—and in turn increase strength and stamina in your muscular system—you must first destroy the muscle fibers you already have? It is only after the literal tearing apart of the muscle fibers that the healing process and production of new and stronger muscle fibers can begin.

An even better example of this concept is the metamorphosis of a butterfly. Have you ever seen what this looks like in its various stages? A few years back, I happened upon the ugliest stage of this taking place on one of my fruit trees in my back acreage. Towards the end of the transition of the metamorphosis process before the caterpillar turns into a butterfly, called the pupa stage, it turns into this black mass of ugliness and death. Looking at it, you would think that there is no way any kind of life could ever come out of something so dark, still, and ugly. Yet, it does, because this is all part of the life cycle of a butterfly. You see, the old creature (caterpillar) must be completely killed in order for the new creation (butterfly) to be brought to life. It's not a transition from an early stage of a creature to the later stage of the creature, it's a transformation from one creation to a completely new creation. However, the caterpillar must be sustained inside a cocoon in order to overcome this process of death and be transformed into a butterfly so that it is protected from outside influences that would rather destroy it than see it gain new life.

The same is true for us. We were created for more than merely surviving and existing in this world; we were created for a life of intimacy with our Creator and others. However, we are all born into a broken world in broken bodies; therefore, overcoming the outside pressures and influences that look to thwart this transformation requires heartache and struggle because it requires death to the old version of you. And in order to survive, we not only need the "cocoon" of a relationship with the Lord, but we also need the "cocoon" of intimate human relationships in order to navigate this transformation process. When our most intimate earthly relationships are with those who understand themselves and the Lord in a deep and true way, we find protection and help to navigate this ugly transformation of the heart that must take place in each of us.

This is how we overcome this messy life and world around us. As a matter of fact, the Word gives us hope and a promise if we choose to trust the process that the Lord has created for us. Jesus tells us in John 16:33, "These things I have spoken to you, that in Me you may have peace. In the world you will have tribulation; but be of good cheer, I have overcome the world." This promise is echoed and expanded upon in 1 John 5:4, which reads, "For whatever is born of God overcomes the world. And this is the victory that has overcome the world—our faith." Anyone who has read even some of the Bible and is familiar with the life and story of Jesus knows that He overcame this world, but that didn't come without tremendous trials, struggles, and heartache. So, think about this with me for a second ... if the perfect Son of God had to go through pain, struggles, trials, and even death in order to triumph over this world, why do we think it would, or should, be any different for us imperfect mortals? The fact is it isn't, but the promise is the hope of a new life on the other side of it. Not only is there an extraordinary beauty in overcoming the harsh realities of this life, but there exists the literal possibility for it to be a reality for each of us if we choose it. This is the hope to which we are called, friends. We may not be able to control all of our circumstances or outcomes in this life, but we are always in control of our perspective and the choices presented to us. So, why not choose hope for something greater?

As I think about God's love in the process of transforming Dave's life, it is clear to me that the Lord needed a long time to soften his heart. This reflection reminds me that although we all must walk the same road for transformation to take place, each of us will travel it at a different pace and therefore, each of us will require different methods along the way.

# CHAPTER FOUR

# God's Methods Are Often Unexpected

When things got to the point with Dave's health that he had to come off the road from his long-haul trucking job and not work at all in February 2023, a month or so later—as the health battle was still raging with signs of progress towards healing but no end in sight—I began asking the Lord to sanctify this situation and show us how He wanted us to walk through this. What was it that He wanted from us in this, and what was it that He wanted from me? If I'm being completely honest, part of this came from a place of desire for total obedience to the Lord, but the larger part came from a place of total frustration and exhaustion. Because at this point in time, just about every area of our lives was under consistent attack due to a choice I had made to step out on the road less traveled a few years back and follow the Lord's specific calling on my life. We were at the point where there was literally nothing left that hadn't been negatively impacted in our reality other than our dogs and physical lives. After asking those questions for a week or so, I remember one day the Lord very clearly saying to me, "I want you to learn to suffer well. This is the call." What!? What does that mean, and why would you want me to suffer, much less suffer well? Although I didn't understand what that meant or what it would look like, I trusted and believed the Lord and the "good word" he had given me for Dave concerning this situation.

During the many hours I spent in prayer for Dave, I heard the Lord tell me a few different times, "Trust me; I've got him. I've got this." The entire time Dave was battling this condition with his kidneys (keep in mind, we didn't know exactly what was happening with his kidneys until September 2023 after we had a biopsy done) the majority of the journey was spent correcting symptoms while trying to figure out what was happening without doing more and/or permanent damage to his body in the process. I truly believed the Lord was going to heal and restore him, and this would be an amazing story that we would be able to share with others one day. Dave believed this too. Turns out, I wasn't wrong; it just looked different than we thought.

My background is eclectic to say the least, and this tends to make me somewhat of an enigma to most people. Like I said in a previous chapter, this girl was born with a little hitch in her giddy up! You see, I have always had diverse interests and passions; while other people seem to instinctively know theirs, I've always struggled to find my true calling. Like I've hinted at previously, I majored in biology with a focus towards medicine, while Dave majored in biology with a focus towards dentistry. I thought and believed that my calling was to be a physician (more specifically, working in ER pediatrics). Most people don't know why I felt this was my calling.

When I lost my dad at the age of thirteen, it impacted me in a profound way. Although I knew my dad had heart disease (this was the diagnosis he had been given), as a young girl, I didn't really understand what that meant or exactly how that played out in the human body. So, after he unexpectedly passed while undergoing an angioplasty at the hospital one day, I became focused on understanding more about the human body. My rationale behind this was to help prevent anyone else from ever experiencing this type of grievous loss. What I didn't know at that young age was this condition is largely reversible with lifestyle changes, but somewhere deep within me, I still knew this should not have happened the way it did.

While studying medicine in college, I found myself struggling to accept many of the concepts being taught in my undergraduate classes regarding the human body, as well as the best methods for working with the challenges and damage that we put our bodies through. It always baffled me that there was so little education given concerning how to maintain a healthy, functioning body, which should include the whole person (mind, body, and spirit). Rather, all the focus was placed on how to treat (not correct) a physical problem once it arose, not to mention that the treatments being taught seemed counterintuitive to how the human body works. And so, I found myself at odds with a few of my professors because I couldn't help but challenge the narratives being taught that didn't align with the reality of human anatomy and physiology. I have never been one to "drink the Kool-Aid" or "go along to get along" just because the power that be said so, and this conviction has only become stronger with each passing year. So, needless to say, I became the outlier who was challenging the official narrative being taught in some of my classes, which led to me failing those classes. Dave and I got married my junior year in college. At this point in time, I began doubting if medicine was the right career path for me, as I had started believing that I was the problem and wasn't smart enough to understand the material being taught. So, all I wanted to do was finish my undergraduate work and then figure out where to go from there.

After my last year at Texas Tech, I moved back to the Dallas–Fort Worth Metroplex, which was home for me. Dave was already living there because he received a job promotion and transferred to the Dallas area during my last year in college. He had taken a management position within the company where he worked, while I was offered a management position at a telecom company. Until I could figure out if I wanted to pursue medical school or not, I decided to take a corporate job with VoiceStream (now T-Mobile). I not only did well in that role but was being groomed for an upper management position within the company, but that wasn't a desire or goal of mine. To be honest, although it had become clear that medicine was not the correct path for me, I still wasn't sure what was. I felt lost. After a couple of years, I left T-Mobile to teach high school, but that didn't feel right either. I also eventually picked up a job at Toyota, which gave me more flexibility and an opportunity to change my career once again. So, I began spending a lot of time in prayer seeking what was next from the Lord, as well as doing some serious introspection about myself and reading various books. During this time, I began the journey down what can only be described as a completely divergent path from anything else that I had ever done: the pursuit of an acting career.

Here is also where I can share some insights into the reason for the strained and difficult relationship with my mom. This background is important to understanding the life path set before me. Something that very few people know and I have never shared with the general public, until now, is that I grew up on film and TV sets. Not because I was an actress myself, but rather, my mom was an actress who pursued a career in the entertainment industry. She always wanted to be famous for acting. It became clear to me, later in life, that this desire of hers came from a misplaced and desperate need for acceptance from others that she had been seeking since childhood. As my mom and I are completely different people, driven by opposite desires in life, I not only had different passions and pursuits than her, but because of the mess and strain that my mom's way of living brought on our family, I wanted to be nothing like her.

As a matter of fact, from a very young age, not only did I want to be completely different than my mom, but I intentionally avoided anything that resembled her. This included clothing, hobbies, and even food choices, as well as a complete aversion—and at times, repulsion—towards the entertainment industry on my part. I never cared about being popular or seen by others as she did—at least, not on a screen. Instead, all I wanted to do was play softball and other sports with my friends, partake in outdoor activities that I enjoyed, spend time with my dad, and just live like all the other kids around me. I may not have been able to voice it in that manner when I was young, but in retrospect, I just wanted to be a "normal kid." However, my mom wanted to push something completely different on me. As you might have already picked up on by now, I was more of a tomboy due to my love of sports and the outdoors, as well as being a daddy's girl through and through. So, anytime my mom tried to push things on me like lace socks, frilly dresses, ribbons for my hair, or anything I perceived as "girly," the answer was an easy and hard no.

As a matter of fact, there is one specific incident that stands out so clearly from my childhood, not only because it paints a perfect picture of this struggle between us, but also because it served to solidify my aversion to my mom and anything she pursued. One summer day, when I was in elementary school (don't remember how old I was, but I know that my dad was still alive and not sick), I remember my mom dragged me to work with her to the set of *Born on the Fourth of July*; they were filming in the InfoMart building in downtown Dallas. You would think most children would be excited to be on a movie set, but on the contrary, I was so pissed that I could have spit nails. Being stuck on that set meant that I'd have to miss out on my softball practice, and that wasn't something I took lightly, considering I had been playing competitively since the age of five. Once we arrived on set, I went over to an empty chair sitting along the all-glass window wall that overlooks Interstate 35, turned it so that my back was towards the set and I was facing the highway, and sat down with the intention of not moving or talking to anyone until it was time to leave. In other words, I was in "full-on sulking mode."

For some reason, the set was shorthanded extras and they were looking for anyone they could to fill in, and they were looking for young kids in particular. Now, my mom's agent at the time was the largest and most respected agent around, not only in the DFW area, but Texas as well. In the past, she had discussed signing me for work with my mom multiple times, as they were convinced I had a look and personality that would make me successful in the industry. But as you might guess, I was not having any of that. So, it came as no surprise that her agent had already told the director of the film that I would make a great child extra for the day, as she and my mom both thought being asked by the director of a major film would be the convincing I needed to finally say yes. I remember my mom coming over trying to convince me, to which I abruptly and adamantly said no. When that didn't work, they sent the director to talk to me; although I don't really remember anything about the conversation, I do know it was short-lived.

When I thought I was home free and could go back to my own world, a man walked up and asked if he could sit in the chair beside me. These people weren't gonna go away easy, and they were willing to pull out all the stops to try and coax me onto the set. So much so that the man they sent to talk to me as the final straw was Tom Cruise. Yep. Tom Cruise was on set that day, and had been all day, unbeknownst to me. Now, keep in mind, Tom was still pretty much an up-and-coming star in the industry at that time, as *Top Gun* was getting him a ton of attention. But other than a familiarity with his name and that he had previously made a popular movie, I really had no idea who he was.

Even though I don't remember all the specifics of our conversation, I remember that he made me feel seen and heard. Tom talked to me like a normal young girl and took the time to get to know a little bit about me. He asked me questions and conversed with me in a way that showed care and concern for me as a person, which I appreciated and continue to respect today. After about ten minutes of chatting and before he left to go back to set, he told me that it was okay for me to continue sitting where I was and that I would be left alone for the rest of the day. As a matter of fact, he personally told the director and crew to leave me alone. That's exactly what happened, as I still had no desire to be in the movie. This wasn't because Tom wasn't enticing and actually almost convincing, but rather, because of the deeply rooted desire to not be like my mom. Plus, Tom said I could!

I share this in order to help you understand why the answer I kept hearing from the Lord to the question, "If not medical school, then what?" not only seemed incorrect, but because it was the exact opposite of what I had been trying to avoid my entire life! You see, I kept hearing the Spirit tell me

I needed to begin pursuing a career in the entertainment industry, more specifically, acting. I didn't understand why the Lord would ever call me into an industry that I perceived as being a weapon of destruction for troubled and broken people like my mom. Please note that I am not saying all people who are drawn to the entertainment industry are troubled and broken, because that's not the case! It's a calling, and many people are made for that type of work. However, what I am saying is that for people such as my mom, this industry is very enticing because it tends to allow them to hide and never deal with their issues.

I also want to be emphatically clear about something. I love my mom—always have and always will. In spite of our vast and distinct differences, there were numerous valuable and positive things my mom taught me that have helped shape who I am today. My heart's desire has always been that she have an abundant life full of joy and peace, and hopefully, to one day have a close mother-daughter relationship like so many of my friends have with their moms. But, the reality is my mom has been a very broken individual most of her life. Unfortunately, because of this (which is not fully, but largely based on choices she made in response to challenges she faced in life), her presence in my life has inadvertently created a toxic emotional, physical, and spiritual environment for me. So, there has always been a need for me to create distinct boundaries in my heart between my mom and me. This made my childhood hard and a relationship with her next to impossible ever since my dad passed.

If you look at my background, it appears as if I am all over the place and don't have a clue as to what I want to do or who I am. I wouldn't argue with that assessment and have even thought that multiple times about my life. However, it is this seemingly discombobulated path with broken family dynamics that has not only shaped me into who I am, but it also, in a way that only God can explain, has prepared me for the "what's next" times in my life.

So, I hope that clarifies why, in 2019, it was such a surprise to me that the Spirit would call me to leave my Toyota job of sixteen years (which was, without a doubt, the best gig I have ever had in regards to money, scheduling, work environment, and flexibility) to pursue an acting career. This new calling to launch a film production company brought serious changes to our lives, and the challenges started rolling in one after another with no apparent end in sight. As a matter of fact, almost two years after I made this change, in August 2020, and under the first year of the COVID pandemic, Dave was laid off from his job of over ten years as a regional trainer for T-Mobile. Now, we were faced with the sobering reality of having lost the sole supporting income of our household while trying to launch a start-up entertainment company.

You see, just because you choose to honor a calling to do the right thing for you, that doesn't mean that the road will be easy or free from detours and land mines. Actually, the opposite is true. Therefore, the question isn't if we will struggle, or how we can avoid it; instead, the question needs to be how will we choose to walk through the struggles and suffering that are bound to come. Because the truth is, suffering is inevitable in this life. The amount of suffering and duration are the only real variables to the equation to which we have any amount of control, and yet, even these can be and often are out of our control. This is where an intimate understanding of the fact that faith and belief are two very different things is necessary. Belief is the initial step, but faith runs much deeper. Faith requires putting your beliefs into action, which always necessitates action on our part.

The truth that suffering is inevitable, as well as a useful tool in the hands of a loving God as a way to bring about good in our lives, has taken on a whole new meaning for me since this all began. As a matter of fact, my outlook on suffering and faith has been forever altered. You see, I have learned that genuine faith in God not only relies on having confidence and hope in what we can't see, but it also requires trust in His timing and methods, which is inexplicably difficult for us mere mortals. At least it is for me.

# CHAPTER FIVE

# Comfort Is the Enemy of Growth

Due to the severe edema that was building up in Dave's body, everyday things became harder and harder for him to do (after the biopsy in September, we discovered that the edema and kidney issues were caused by a rare autoimmune disorder he acquired called focal segmented glomerularsclerosis, or FSGS for short). But we kept seeking and trusting the Lord to provide what Dave needed to get through this and see us to the other side. However, as the months passed, he steadily put on more weight and became increasingly less capable of accomplishing everyday tasks such as taking a shower on his own or walking from the living room to the bedroom without running out of breath due to the edema in his chest pressing against his lungs. There would be moments where he would just start weeping, and at his wits' end, he'd say to me, "My body can't take much more of this. It's so hard. When is this going to end?" Hearing and seeing this broke my heart, but I kept reminding him that the Lord would get us through this. I would tell him I didn't know why the Lord was allowing all of this to continue, but it seemed like the Lord's plan was the long game on this one, and we just had to stay the course, to which Dave always agreed and kept fighting. Because the truth is the Lord was sustaining him during this time.

The day we had to make the call to take Dave to the hospital for the first time was October 7, 2023. That was Dave's forty-eighth birthday, and the previous night had been the roughest, yet greatest night of this journey up to that point. The reason was because in the pain, exhaustion, and frustration, we were both struggling to deal and keep going, and I began to really crack for the first time. I remember late that evening as Dave was sitting in the leather chair in our living room and we were discussing the reality of the lack of any sustainable progress towards healing, I fell to my knees and face on the floor and began crying, pounding the floor, and screaming "I can't do this anymore!" It wasn't because I was angry at Dave, but rather just frustrated, exhausted, and angry in general that things weren't changing for the better even though we were doing everything we knew to do. I just couldn't understand why God wasn't moving and changing his situation for us. This caused Dave to break. Throughout this entire process, Dave would constantly tell me that I was his rock, and he leaned on me to keep pushing through this.

In that moment, he broke down from exhaustion and frustration as well, which eventually led to him sharing a very personal struggle that the Lord had been dealing with him about this entire time. It was in that moment of sharing and hearing my response that healing and freedom took place for Dave. Freedom from long-held bondage over his life that I never really knew about prior to this moment. It was at this point, because of the freedom that came from confessing it and the willingness on my part to receive what he shared with love and forgiveness, that I began to see a new creation coming to life in him. He was a transformed man with a different heart. From this time forward until his last day, I saw the sheer pleasure and peace in his face when he was spending time with the Lord in prayer or worship through music (which he did multiple times a day), as well as a different countenance the rest of the time: He was more understanding, patient, and tender-hearted towards everyone than he had ever been. Don't get me wrong; this doesn't mean that he didn't get frustrated, ask God "Why won't you heal me?" or lose his patience in a moment of frustration, but those were the exceptions, not the norm.

You see, the Lord had been teaching both of us a great deal over those months about what it truly means to "choose justice, love mercy, and walk humbly with your God," which is the call of God for each of us, according to the Bible. This is how and why I was able to show grace and forgiveness so readily to Dave for what he shared. The fact is that from Genesis to Revelation, the path that the Lord has chosen for us is centered around entering into his rest. He wants to give each of us an abundant life centered on rest in the Lord (rest for your mind, heart, soul, and body).

Believe it or not, the path to the rest mentioned above in the eulogy lies in learning to become comfortable with the uncomfortable. Sounds oxymoronic, I know, but this concept is true for many things in life, and I'll share why I believe this is the case in a minute. A good parallel that helps depict this concept is the hatching process of chickens. Anyone who knows me would not at all be surprised that I am mentioning chickens in this book; if anything, they're probably surprised it took me this long to mention them since I love my "hot mess express" of a chicken clan. Just to set the record straight, not only are chickens some of the funniest animals ever created, but they are smart too, at least sometimes. I know ... they are chickens, so before some of you lose it altogether, I'm not talking about Mensa status here, so you can stay calm and cluck on. But I can tell you for a fact that chickens are very aware of their surroundings and understand more than you think, even the sound of their name. Before I go too far down this rabbit trail, let's get back to why I mentioned chickens in the first place.

At the beginning of this year (early January 2025), I had the bright idea to see if my "accidental rooster" could add more to this homestead than his daily crowing and self-appointed body guard status over the hens, as well as I wanted to know if Pancake (yes, my rooster's name is Pancake) was shooting blanks or not. So, I decided to incubate four eggs from the hens I knew Pancake recently "had his way with." Not to mention, I had lost three hens from the clan over the previous year and a half, so I needed to recuperate the egg production that was lost. Since acquiring my own chickens, I have come to understand some important aspects of the hatching process. In order for a chicken to hatch in the natural manner, the mother hen must sit on top of her egg for the entire incubation period, which is between twenty-one and twenty-three days, until the chick hatches. So, unless I wanted to lose the ability to acquire farm fresh eggs from four of my nine hens, I needed to find another way to hatch some chicks. January is the perfect time to hatch chicks because this means they will be laying eggs by late spring. Now, keep in mind, just because an egg gets fertilized doesn't mean that a chicken will hatch. That only happens if and when the egg undergoes the very rigid and controlled process of incubation. With that said and after some in-depth research, I found an incubator online that was perfect. It would allow me to keep a controlled environment of every aspect required during the incubation period for the eggs, while keeping a close eye on them at the same time.

So, when the morning of the final day of incubation, day twenty-one, had finally arrived, I was excited but a little nervous to see if any of the eggs had life in them. Honestly, I thought none of the eggs were going to hatch, not because I hadn't done everything needed over the past twenty days but because whenever I looked at the eggs through the candler, there was no sign of life in any of them. Out of the four eggs incubated, only one was white and the other three were various shades of blue and green. I was only able to see through the white egg, which never showed any signs of life. So, my expectations were minimal, but I was still holding out hope for the other three. Needless to say, when I looked in the incubator that morning and saw a crack in one of the blue eggs, I was thankful that I didn't listen to the voice in my head telling me to give up and just toss them!

From my research, I learned that the hatching process begins with the chicks creating a crack or hole in the egg shell. Now, the process of hatching, from the initial crack to coming out of the shell, can take anywhere from five to twenty-four hours depending on the strength and health of the chick. As you might imagine, this is an exhausting and arduous process for the chicks. Ideally, they should not have any outside help to make this happen, even in nature. This process was amazing to watch. My first chick born, CJ (Clueless Jr.), took about five hours total from the appearance of the first hole until he was fully hatched. However, as I was looking at the remaining two colored eggs that might have been fertilized, I didn't see any signs of life, which left me unsure of what to do since we were on day twenty-one. Knowing that some eggs can hatch on day twenty-two, I decided to keep incubating the remaining eggs overnight, just in case. As I was checking on the eggs later that night, I noticed something. One of the remaining easter eggs was rocking back and forth. Then, all of a sudden, I heard some chirping that sounded as if it was coming from the incubator. So, I leaned in closer to the clear dome cover to look, and as I was asking my mom if she heard the chirping, there it was once more. This time, I was able to determine the source of the chirping as the egg that was rocking back and forth. So, like only a crazy girl who is accustomed to talking to herself because she is an actress who rehearses out loud for auditions does, I began telling the baby chick, "Keep going, little girl. You can do it. We're waiting for you!" It took everything I had to not open that incubator and help create a hole for this little girl to hatch because it was clear she was struggling. I think this may have been why she was chirping. You see, this egg was from one of my chickens (Lady) whose eggs have much thicker shells, which meant this little girl was going to have a fight on her hands to get out of there. That also probably explained why she was a day late in hatching. Little Ginger (I named her Ginger, with the help and suggestion from friends, because of her color and due to her spicy attitude ...) had started rocking and pecking the evening of day twenty-one, but she did not fully hatch until early afternoon on day twenty-two. This process took her almost a full twenty-four hours: much longer than CJ.

The hatching process is not only extremely uncomfortable for the chick, but it is an intense struggle of survival because the chick must do it on its own with no outside help, if possible. If it doesn't have the strength and fortitude to survive this very trying process, then the likelihood that it will survive all the pressures of this world become slim to none. Friends, in a similar way, the same is true with us. Struggles, trials, and pain are the tools that God uses to shape our character, and a main way that we are able to defeat the enemies of our soul.

There were many lessons the Lord taught Dave and me during his health battle, but one lesson in particular that I want to share with you is in regards to this aspect of becoming comfortable with the uncomfortable. We learned this key concept from our amazing brother in the Lord, Jamie Walden; he taught us that there is a big difference between surrender and submission. Once again, please hear my heart. My desire is not to push belief in the Lord or faith on you. Like everyone, I can only share from my personal experiences and knowledge. So, for those of you reading this who may not believe in God or in having a personal relationship with the Lord, I ask you to consider this perspective, as it offers a point of view that can still teach you something about the world. It's worth considering because I believe understanding this distinction is critical to true growth and "right" living before our Creator and relationally with one another in this world. As Jamie so aptly describes it: The command and call on the lives of those who choose to place their faith in God (the saints) is to submit to the Lord because in submission, there is freedom, but in surrender, there is war and chaos. Like me, maybe some of you can relate to war and chaos in your heart and mind at one point in time or another.

The distinction between the two is the key, and it's something that I had never even considered until I heard Jamie talking about it one day. A seasoned war fighter with many years of combat experience as a Marine who has seen this played out on a modern battlefield, Jamie clearly lays out the difference between surrender and submission in war. Listen to his words, friends.

> Surrender is a matter of the will. When someone surrenders, they are disarmed, but allowed to retain their identity, norms, and customs. When someone surrenders, they yield themselves to the power controlling them through compulsion or demand. They yield their will to another out of necessity and desperation. Those who surrender retain a sense of identity, national origin, and always retain pride. They retain a sense of self. It's characterized by resentment, retention of pride, distrust, and an internalized willful defiance to the one exercising power and authority over them. It is self-protective. It assumes oppression; therefore, it will always resist. Those who surrender will never assimilate. They retain their identity until the day they die as an enemy combatant. Surrender is a matter of the will based on defeat, and looks like a SERE operation (which stands for survive, evade, resist, and escape).
>
> But submission, on the other hand, is a matter of the heart. Submission is a condition of being humble and compliant. It is a willful and deliberate choice. It is not imposed by force. In submission, one chooses to come underneath the authority of another with no form of resentment

or pride. One who submits entrusts themselves to the one exercising power and authority over them. They trust their leadership, even if they don't agree or understand. The posture of submission is humble, quiet, servant-minded, and it seeks the good of the one to whom it is entrusted. Submission does not desire rebellion, to overthrow, or to escape. It wholeheartedly assimilates. Those who submit are considered trusted confidants who share in the depth of unity with the one whom they have submitted themselves to because submission is a matter of the heart.

You see, Dave had finally come to a place of submission before the Lord versus a place of mere surrender, and the Lord was able to complete a mighty work in his heart and life because of it. It was absolutely beautiful to watch this play out in his life. The Lord was also teaching me how to come to this same place as well.

I'm not saying that this journey has been easy, fun, or in any way desirable. It's been the exact opposite, but I believe learning to become comfortable with the uncomfortable in this life is the calling of the Lord for each of us, as it is the path to the abundant life he has for all of us. We all will choose to surrender or submit to something in this life. The only question for each of us is to whom or what that will be.

This life is a process, and on this journey, there will be highs and lows, heartache and joy, peace and discomfort. At times, we will have a beautiful mountain-top view, while at other times, we will be in the valley of despair with only a shadow of something lost hovering over us. How we choose to respond to the uncomfortable is the only choice each of us really has in this area, and the choice we make determines whether we overcome or are overcome by the challenges of this life.

# CHAPTER SIX

# Your Choices Determine Your Experience

The call to learn to "suffer well" for us in this was a call to willingly choose to allow the Lord to crush the Egypt in our hearts (literally beat the hell out of our corrupt and broken flesh), so that He would be able to properly create eternity in our spirits, and we could properly reflect the God of the Bible. In my opinion and experience, this is the only place where true freedom and life are found. This may sound like a depressing and undesirable word to some of you, but Dave would tell you that it is actually just the opposite, friends!

He taught me many things over the years, but the greatest lesson Dave ever taught me in this life was how to suffer well—something I am still in the process of learning. Dave never saw himself as someone whom the Lord used in significant ways in this world. He would often say to me, "I'm not able to teach other people," which wasn't true at all, or "I don't have the ability to lead other people spiritually," or "How do my gifts and talents impact this world and others in a meaningful way?" But what he never saw and understood was how much his life and actions spoke more about who the Lord is and what is truly important in this life than mere words ever could.

This was especially evident in the last months and days of his life. I watched an entire floor of hospital staff show concern, care, extra attention, and daily discussion about his condition (even the nurses and doctors who did not treat him) because of the impression he made on them all. I watched the dialysis nurses dote and love on him and ask us about our marriage. They wanted to know what made us so different from the other people they saw and treated. They were all so amazed that I was by his side twenty-four seven and advocated on his behalf during this time, which dumbfounded me because my only thought and response to this was, "This is my other half. Where else would I be?" I watched his nephrologist team (especially his nephrologist in the hospital) work hand-in-hand with us and honor our decisions to try and remain pure before the Lord in every medical decision we made as we walked this journey towards physical healing. Dave would tell me, "You have been and are an angel sent to me; you are my rock, and I couldn't do this without you. You are such a blessing, especially during all of this." But for me, the truth was he was my rock because even when he wanted to quit due to the physical pain being literally more than he could bear, he kept going. He fought with a smile on his face, and expressed kind and grateful words to all those around him who helped and served him during this time. Once again, he was teaching me what it looked like to choose to "suffer well." He had truly come to a place of complete submission before the Lord in this, and acceptance of whatever the Lord chose to do, even if it wasn't what he wanted. This was apparent and clear all the way to the end.

The thing that kept reverberating in my brain as I was reading this section is that we play an active role in all of our experiences in life, whether we realize it or not. How and why this is the case is what vexes most of us. Let me help you understand what I mean by this.

In full transparency, this chapter has been the hardest and taken me the longest to complete, as not only is it still hard for me to rehash the details of this experience due to the strong emotions it evokes within me, but I also realize it might feel uncomfortable for those reading it to accept the possibility behind the story being told. It's important to read this chapter with the understanding that it is about sharing the truth around what we experienced and uncovered during Dave's medical journey, as well as what the Lord has shown me through this experience. So, my hope and prayer is that you are able to receive the words that are shared in the spirit from which they are written, which is a desire to connect with each of you in an authentic and loving way, while remaining firmly planted in the truth of our journey. With that said, I encourage you to allow this story to continue to unfold authentically with eyes of grace. If you are feeling brave and ready, maybe even (like I have had to do with myself over these past few years) be willing to scrutinize and challenge your personally held beliefs to ensure that you are moving forward in a healthy and abundant life rooted in truth.

You see, our experiences don't necessarily equate to truth; they equate to our reality, and reality isn't always based in truth. I have seen this play out in my life many times and in many ways over the years. Think about it with me for a moment. Although our feelings and emotions are real (and should not be discounted or minimized in any way) and the circumstances we face are real, this doesn't mean that what we are feeling about the circumstances is rooted in truth. Let me give you an example of what I mean. For many years of my life, I had an intense fear of flying. In the beginning when I started flying for work, the fear was so bad that without some type of convincing reassurance to the contrary, I would spend the entire flight fearful that we might crash. Needless to say, I hated turbulence of any kind. I remember one flight in particular where my neuroses got the best of me. One day, as I was walking onto the plane, for some unplanned reason and with zero hesitation, I chose to turn left towards the open cockpit door and have a quick chat with the pilots. To the best of my memory, my uninhibited self decided to say to them something along these lines, "Good morning. Hopefully, you are both well-rested and awake. I need you to look right here (pointing to my eyes). Remember, my life is in your hands. So, stay alert, and if we encounter turbulence *of any kind,* please look for alternative altitudes to get us out of it. Also, keep us informed of any changes or issues during the flight. I would greatly appreciate it *guys.*" Then, I turned and calmly headed out of the cockpit to my seat as if this was the normal boarding process. These kind pilots humored me during the flight. After we reached our cruising altitude, the pilots sent a note with one of the flight attendants back to me asking how they were doing. Then, halfway through the flight, the captain stepped out of the cockpit and came to find me on his way to the bathroom. He wanted to see if the flight was smooth enough, and if I was okay with everything thus far. It had been a very smooth flight, which I gladly let him know.

Now, why would I ever do such a thing? (Other than the fact that my drummer marches sideways.) I did this with no pause or thought of just how irrational it was because I was allowing a paralyzing fear of crashing to grip my heart and control my thoughts and actions. Was what I was feeling real to me in the moment? Absolutely. However, these feelings and this thought process that caused the fear were not being informed by facts about the flight that took place before or during the flight to warrant such feelings and behavior, but rather, they came from the irrational and erroneous emotions controlling my thoughts about a situation that I had no control over. The truth was that I feared the lack of control that I had in this situation.

As humans, we tend to unwittingly use our feelings as a compass to guide us to truth, when, in actuality, it should be the opposite: Truth should be the compass that helps direct our feelings. Keep in mind that for most of us, our feelings change as often as our underwear (which is daily ... hopefully), and that can happen multiple times a day, depending on what we are experiencing, right? Therefore, feelings always have been and always will be a by-product of our experiences in this life. Hence the saying "Discover your true north." Just because our experiences in life will vary from person to person does not mean that truth can vary from person to person. Did you know there is a difference between what is called magnetic north and true north when using a compass? *True north* refers to the geographic North Pole, and is, therefore, fixed. It is constant. Whereas magnetic north aligns with Earth's magnetic field, which shifts over time. Consequently, it is not constant, and therefore, is not a good gauge to correctly guide someone because it can be manipulated by outside forces. In other words, you shouldn't bank on it. I have already stated but it warrants being repeated, I do not want to minimize or negate someone's feelings because feelings are real and powerful things that we must own and acknowledge, as they are designed to be a physical expression of something occurring within our inner being that should always be given the proper attention. But, I do believe that respectfully acknowledging and confronting the truth of our emotions should not be mutually exclusive. They can and should coexist in each of us in order to be a healthy and balanced human being.

Merriam-Webster defines *truth* as: the body of real things, events, and facts: actuality. The very meaning of the word lets us know that truth can't be subjective, but rather, it must be objective, or else there is no standard by which to measure what is not true. Because of this, truth can't originate from people because people are imperfect beings; we're flawed by nature. So, truth must originate from an outside source other than humans. However, what can, does, and will vary from person to person is what we accept and hold as truth in our hearts. Each of us has the God-given right to choose what this is for ourselves. But what we often fail to recognize is that our choices always have consequences, to the good and the bad. More importantly, our choices not only have consequences for our lives, but they also can directly impact the lives of those around us, to the good and the bad. As humans, we are prone to avoid hearing and receiving this for one simple reason: It brings a level of personal accountability for our choices to the equation. Personal accountability is a necessary precept that largely appears to have been lost in our society, which is dangerous because the concept "you reap what you sow" was written into the very fabric of every aspect of this world by our Creator. This is very similar to the concept that people refer to as *karma*. Therefore, it is unavoidable, no matter how we feel about it.

Now that I've laid the conceptual foundation, here is where the discussion gets raw and real concerning Dave's story for a moment, friends. So far, I've spent this book sharing with you some details about how the condition Dave acquired (FSGS) impacted our lives in specific ways, but until now, I have never shed light on how this condition began. I need to point out that Dave was a physically fit and active man who never had any major illness or hospital stay, other than an emergency appendectomy at the age of thirteen, his entire life until this happened. We both chose to live based on a holistic approach to our overall health.

Since it's difficult to know exactly where to start in a story with a million moving parts, let me begin by saying that November 2019 was the initiation of a change in everything for us, even though we had no idea at the time. Looking back on it now, I realize we weren't the only ones who would be impacted from what was taking place around our world. These changes would impact every human being on the planet in a way that nothing else ever has, at least not in our lifetime. Even though I don't believe it is healthy at all to center your life around any political landscape, for me, it has always been important to, at the very least, remain aware of what is taking place politically in the US, as well as globally. Mainly because it impacts most aspects of our daily lives. So, in November 2019, when all the chaos surfaced with the US election results, which seemingly coincided with a new global pandemic that was burgeoning on the scene, let's just say my "Spidey senses" went on high alert. As someone who has spent years receiving education and training on the human body, nothing I kept hearing and seeing was making any sense, especially in regards to this pandemic. Dave and I were on the same page with this, which was a blessing. The official narrative blasted via the media, pictures, and videos being shared, and the lack of confirmation concerning the necessary and scientific evidence to prove the narrative bombarding society not only made us want to pause, but hit the brakes altogether while we did a deep dive into the validity of it all. So, that's exactly what we did. After all, isn't this the most rational approach to take, especially with something as high stakes as your health and life? Due to our in-depth knowledge/background of the human body, as well as our deep-seated faith, it didn't take long for both of us to come to the conclusion that something much bigger than a virus was at play here, and from what we could ascertain, nothing surrounding the situation appeared to have our best interests in mind. With that said, we both made the decision to follow what we knew was true according to science and our faith in God versus allowing the fear that, from our perspective, was clearly and intentionally being perpetrated to guide our decision-making process. Among the things we did and didn't do during this time, neither of us got vaccinated.

What has been the most heartbreaking to me about this whole situation is watching the division, animosity, and destruction that this one choice has brought into the lives of people all over the world, including ours. Like many of you reading this, we had family and friends who took an opposite stance from us on this. We have all seen how being on different sides of this so-called debate (once again, an unnecessary debate that was created and dumped on society as a whole, as this should be an individual choice) has literally torn relationships, families, and lives apart at the seams. Let me clearly state that I wholeheartedly believe in an individual's right to choose what goes into their body; it's called medical freedom. It always has been and always should be an individual's choice ... period. Now, for those of you who right now might be thinking, "Vicki, I didn't have a choice. I didn't want to take it, but I would have lost my job if I didn't," or "I had to take it in order to protect those around me who were at risk," or any of the many other reasons people choose to take it, my goal here is not to change someone's stance on this topic, or shame someone who chose differently than us. That's not the purpose of this story or book, nor the desire of my heart. Along those same lines, neither Dave nor I held any animosity or resentment towards those who chose differently than us. Nevertheless, it is necessary to point out that whatever someone's reasoning to take or not take it, at the end of the day, it was and is a choice on our part, especially since (to my knowledge) no law was ever instituted anywhere requiring this for anyone. I always have and always will respect someone's choice, even if I don't agree with it. Being able to get along with and show respect to people from all walks of life is a basic requirement. But what perplexes me to this day is why society as a whole continues to push back against open and honest discussions regarding vaccinations (which is what we are doing right now) and acknowledging it as being an individual's choice? When did a mutual respect for others, having dialogue regarding varying opinions, and being able to "agree to disagree" with people of differing viewpoints become a relic of the past? We must find our way back to at least some resemblance of this in order to maintain healthy and functioning relationships within society.

Why take the time to mention all of this, and what does it have to do with Dave's story? Well, I believe the timing of Dave's sudden acquiring of this autoimmune condition is in perfect alignment with many known side effects of the COVID pandemic.

As I shared in a previous chapter, after Dave was let go from his corporate job with T-Mobile under the COVID lockdown frenzy in August 2020, he eventually took a long-haul trucking job beginning in October 2021. One year into the job, I received a text one morning that disturbed me enough to call him. He had sent me a picture of his face, and it was so swollen that I could barely see his eyes. His face looked like a Shar-Pei! As we were talking, Dave said the only thing he could imagine that might have caused it was an allergic reaction of some sort. At the time, he was driving through the Midwest transporting beef, so he thought it might be due to the various pollens blowing in the air out that way, but that didn't make sense to me. He had never experienced this severe of a reaction just from allergies or pollen prior to this, so why now? However, by the time I called him back, he had been awake and driving for a few hours and the swelling in his face had gone away completely. So, in typical Dave fashion, he wasn't worried about it any longer. Although I still had my reservations and concern regarding this, I decided to trust his instincts and just asked him to let me know if it happens again.

Within a few days of this event, Dave called me one morning and said that he was having severe swelling in his legs and feet by the end of each day, and the only way that he was able to relieve the swelling was to lay down and elevate his legs at night, which was now part of his daily routine. He also told me that he had woken up at 5 a.m. that morning with pain in his lower abdomen and sides. It was at this point in time that he asked me to pray for the situation, as he felt he might have developed kidney stones. Not a fun situation for anyone ever, much less when you're driving twelve to fourteen hours a day for work!

Mind you, even though he drove and lived in a truck on the road when working, he made sure to drink plenty of water daily, and made his own food to ensure he was eating as clean and healthy as possible. He did the best he could to keep as close to the same eating habits as we had at home. So, it wasn't as if he was drinking and eating junk during this time, even if it would have been much easier to do.

As he was keeping me in the loop and we were working together to figure out what was happening in his body, he implemented various proven, all-natural effective protocols to help his kidneys and liver, as he felt that he couldn't afford to come off the road; his pay was directly linked to the number of miles he drove. If he didn't drive, he didn't get paid. Not to mention, we had no health insurance with this job, as the company did not pay to cover any of the insurance, so we opted out of it. We had gone stretches before with no health insurance, which never concerned us because we were both so healthy. Things continued this way for a few months, and the various protocols he was following seemed to help keep the visible symptoms from getting worse, but they weren't correcting them or getting him closer to healing. Early in this process, we both noticed that it made a huge difference in alleviating the swelling in his feet and legs when he got to come home in between trips to lie down and elevate his feet for a day or two. However, as soon as he was back up walking, standing, or sitting for any length of time, the swelling would come right back. In addition to this, taking daily hot Epsom salt baths helped pull out some of the edema, and subsequently, allowed him to shed three to five pounds each time he did this. We thought that maybe this was going to be the process we'd follow as his body worked to break up and pass the kidney stone(s) that seemed to exist. However, after months of doing this, we noticed that not only was he beginning to struggle with keeping the edema from getting any worse, but the situation wasn't healing him enough.

It all culminated in two different instances of Dave passing kidney stones while he was on the road. After the first time he passed some stones, Dave told me that he felt better and thought the problem had been fixed. Later that same week, as he was driving from Oklahoma to San Antonio, Dave planned a stop near our house so we could eat dinner together. He had me meet him in a parking lot near our house with dinner. He looked and sounded much better with less swelling, so I thought we were in the clear. But it was only three hours into his drive after dinner that I received a phone call telling me that the severe pain was back. He was trying to pass another kidney stone, and this time, the pain was much worse. I told him that it was time to turn around and come home, to which he agreed. For Dave to agree to come home, I knew it was bad.

The plan was for me to meet him at the truck yard once he got there and help him fully unload his truck, since he didn't know when he would be able to go back to work. When Dave originally called me, he was just on the other side of Waco, which is about two hours away from us. Needless to say, that was the longest two hours of his life! Once he arrived, I learned that he had pain and nausea the entire drive back, and he vomited twice while driving. The pain and nausea didn't subside until about five minutes before he pulled into the lot. We immediately sought out a urologist, and discovered that he did indeed have kidney stones. The doctor said he most likely passed multiple kidney stones a few different times. Even though he wasn't experiencing any of the pain and nausea he had been while on the road, the swelling was still there. We learned this was due to the fact that Dave had a kidney stone the shape of an upside down snowman lodged at the top of the ureter of his right kidney. This was not only almost impossible to pass on his own, but even if he could, it would hurt like a mother. So, we chose to go with the recommendation of having a ureteroscopy done before this stone started to move or break up on its own.

We had the procedure done within a few days of the urologist appointment. The surgery went well. The urologist was able to remove all of the kidney stones, and Dave spent two and a half weeks at home resting and recovering. During this time, all of the swelling eventually subsided, and his weight had almost returned back to normal. He was looking and feeling better than he had in months, and there were no signs of any stones left or new stones developing. We were thankful for the healing, but Dave was itching to get back to work. He had planned his return to the road on a Wednesday, as he was on the road to a full recovery.

The next part of the story is where things gets complicated and hard for people to understand. Especially in the early days of the pandemic, there was nothing but chaos and confusion for society as a whole. But, because the purpose of this book is to lend a helping hand and offer hope to those who are lost due to deep pain and suffering, the details of exactly how Dave acquired this autoimmune condition are better suited for a different setting (one in which I will gladly share with anyone interested). With that said, here's what you need to know. For the first time since the pandemic began in 2020, I got sick after being in a large group setting one Sunday and developed all the hallmark symptoms of what the scientific community calls the effects of a COVID-related illness; body aches/pains, extreme tiredness, and overall weakness kept me in bed for days. Once I realized that I had caught something (Monday morning), I ensured that I kept my distance from Dave in an attempt to keep him well so he could return to work on the following Wednesday. As you can rightly assume, we were too late. He had already caught a COVID-related illness from me.

It literally only took twenty-four hours after he went back out on the road for the leg and feet swelling and subsequent weight gain to stage a comeback. However, this time, there was no kidney pain or new kidney stones involved. So, Dave was assuming that it was due to going back to sitting for twelve to fourteen hours a day in that driver's seat after having a major procedure done. He thought maybe he hadn't allowed his body and immune system enough time to recuperate. He didn't initially equate catching this illness from me as being the driving force behind this resurgence because he had what the scientific community called COVID at the beginning of the pandemic, from which he made a full recovery. Plus, the kidney stones had been removed, which was what caused all these issues the first time. All of this took place shortly after Thanksgiving in 2022.

In February 2023, Dave came off the road permanently with the hopes that a strict regimen of rest and elevating his feet would be the key to his healing once more. Like I mentioned in the eulogy portion from chapter 5, it wasn't until September of 2023, after getting a biopsy done, that we discovered that Dave had FSGS (focal segmented glomerular-sclerosis), which effects less than 3 percent of the population.

In the simplest terms possible, FSGS causes scarring of the glomeruli: the small parts of the kidney that filter waste from the blood. This scarring prevents the kidneys from filtering the blood properly, which, in turn, leads to protein being lost via urine, instead of absorbed into the bloodstream, while the waste products in the blood seep out of the blood vessels into the interstitial fluid of the body. This seepage is what causes the edema, and when this edema builds up for a long period, blood-borne infections can occur. It was both edema and blood-borne infections that landed Dave in the hospital for the first time in October 2023. According to many health experts, the fallout from this thing attacking our bodies labeled COVID was so outside the "normal range" of how viruses work that it was literally attacking multiple organs within the body of those affected, in particular, the heart, lungs, liver, kidneys, and reproductive organs. Since his kidneys were weakened at the time of exposure, this is what we believed these foreign substances attacked, and what began the downhill spiral of Dave's health.

Although easy to do, it would be disingenuous and shortsighted of me as a person of faith to say that this was the sole reason for Dave's passing. I believe that life is the sum of our choices. I also believe that the number of our days on this Earth are determined before we are ever born. The first is in our control, and the second is in the hands of the Lord. Because of this, the Lord can and will use whatever He chooses to bring about His ultimate plan for our lives, which always has our best interests in mind.

Please stay with me here, I am not saying that our choices don't impact the direction of our lives or even the outcome of things in this life; they absolutely do! Therefore, we are not called to just sit by and "let life happen to us." Instead, the message I am trying to convey was put in motion before the creation of the world, and that it is almost impossible for our human minds to comprehend. It is best summed up in one of my favorite Bible passages, Isaiah 55:8–9: "'For My thoughts are not your thoughts, Nor are My ways your ways,' says the Lord. 'For as the heavens are higher than the earth, so are My ways higher than your ways, and My thoughts than your thoughts.'" Only a divine, loving, and sovereign Creator can take the good and the bad of this life and use both to accomplish what He has planned for us, as He alone knows the end from the beginning. I believe this was the case with Dave. Yes; this autoimmune condition played a huge role in his passing, but hindsight has revealed to me that there were multiple things all working together that ultimately led to this outcome. Friends, it is never as simple as just one thing in these situations, it is a culmination of circumstances (some out of our control), life choices, and the timing of a sovereign God.

Due to the nature of how drastic the protocol in medicine seemed to change overnight with the onset of this worldwide pandemic, Dave and I wanted to avoid the hospital at all costs, if possible. We did so up until October 7, 2023. As I revealed in the eulogy excerpt from chapter 5, that was Dave's forty-eighth birthday, and one of our dear friends, Brad Powers, who had loved Dave so well, stopped by to visit and bring him some birthday presents. We spent the first half of the day watching the Texas Tech football game and celebrating his birthday with Brad. Within twenty minutes of Brad leaving, Dave began complaining about a specific pain in his abdomen and thighs, which was new, but what we believed at the time was most likely linked to sitting in the reclining chair for too long. So, I started doing lymphatic massage on his legs, as this was something I did every night on his entire body to help offer relief from the pain caused by the edema. However, this wasn't bringing him any relief, as it usually did. We were both getting frustrated at this point because we had no idea what to do. After about ten minutes of a back-and-forth discussion on what to do, I finally lifted up his shirt and lowered his sleep pants in order to take a look at his abdomen and thighs. As soon as I did, it was clear that we had to take him to the hospital. The discoloration in his upper thigh and lower abdomen on his right side let me know that he most likely had a blood infection. (This had shown up on his body sometime in the afternoon, as it was not there that morning.) It didn't take long in the ER for their evaluation to reveal that he needed to be checked into the hospital for treatment. Dave spent sixteen days in the hospital during this visit. Because I knew the importance of monitoring every single thing taking place with his health during this time, I decided to stay at the hospital the entire time—the cafe staff and many of the X-ray and sonogram technicians knew me by name. This decision was key if Dave was going to be able to leave the hospital.

Although there were many battles that unfolded for me during those sixteen days on Dave's behalf, two in particular stand out in my mind. You see, my background had instilled in me the importance of remaining aware and vigilant with all procedures and medications being administered during any hospital visit. As any of the nurses and doctors who treated Dave would tell you, I made it a point to be in his room when shift change occurred each day in order to talk to the doctors and nurses working his case. I would have them go through the list of medications he would be receiving with the dosage so that I could confirm whether or not he would take them. This saved his life a few times.

Within the first twenty-four hours of checking Dave into the hospital, his nephrologist had discussed with us his condition and the safest approach to start trying to reverse it, while working to alleviate as much of the edema as possible. We had reluctantly agreed to a pretty high dose of steroids on a daily basis back in September after his biopsy, as this was the standard protocol for treating FSGS. The majority of patients who had this condition and were prescribed the steroids noticed improvements. At our wits' end and with this being the option with the least amount of risk and side effects (that's saying a lot when 40 mg of a steroid each day is the option with the least amount of side effects), Dave agreed to try it. With that said, we adamantly refused any blood pressure or cholesterol medication that had been recommended, as not only did science not show any conclusive evidence that this supports the kidneys, but also because we knew the facts behind the serious side effects and harm that these medications wreak on the body's filtering organs, which is a great deal of risk with very little, if any, reward. So, needless to say, when the nurses and doctors would list a blood pressure medication as one of his meds, we immediately refused it.

The first main battle we fought had to do with one of Dave's new medications. During this time, he was on a few different antibiotics and antifungal IV medications for the blood-borne infection, and in order to begin reversing the severe edema, we agreed to try an IV Lasix medication. (Dave was five eleven with a healthy weight around 180 pounds. When he was checked into the hospital on October 7, he weighed in at 310 pounds! He was carrying almost the equivalent of his entire body weight in edema, and it was everywhere!) Dave had only tried one Lasix pill previously to no avail, and this was prior to the biopsy where we learned exactly what was taking place with his kidneys. Using any type of Lasix medication with certain kidney conditions can cause more damage and even lead to kidney failure. So, we had been looking to avoid these issues and use extreme caution if and when it became necessary.

It was around 10:30 p.m. on his first night in the hospital, as I was laying down on the couch in Dave's room almost asleep, that he called for me. He told me he wasn't feeling right, and hadn't been for a few hours at that point. Although I don't clearly remember all the symptoms he was having, as he was telling me about them, it was clear that something had changed in his condition. Prior to this moment, the pain he had been experiencing before we arrived to the hospital had subsided. As we were talking and trying to figure out why this was happening, I ran through his medicine list once more. It was then that we realized the only new thing that had been introduced was the Lasix. This IV had been started just a few hours earlier. So, we immediately knew this is what was causing his issues.

We called for his nurse and informed her that we wanted the IV to be stopped. The nurse was very caring and understood why we were asking for this after we explained everything to her, but due to protocol, she couldn't stop the IV without approval from the doctor on call that night. So, we had to wait for the doctor to come by the room. Once the doctor arrived and heard our request and reasons behind it, the doctor proceeded to explain why she couldn't do it. However, I kept advocating for his right as a patient to make whatever medical decision he deemed right for himself. After she argued with us for about fifteen more minutes, I finally said that if she didn't stop the IV right now, I would do it myself. I also told her that we would take full responsibility for this decision, and she could tell his nephrologist as much. So, she acquiesced to our request.

Within thirty minutes of stopping the IV, the symptoms Dave was experiencing went away completely, and he was able to sleep. When his nephrologist made her rounds the following morning, as we were discussing what happened and why we chose to do what we did, she agreed with the call we made. Come to find out, this particular IV Lasix will only work to achieve what our goal was when it is used with another infusion simultaneously, which they didn't do. I can only imagine the condition Dave would have been in if we would have allowed the IV to continue running until the nephrologist arrived the following morning.

The second critical battle we fought in the hospital was in regards to the decision about whether or not to take a blood transfusion. The only reason we even had to consider this was because after we realized that IV Lasix wasn't an option to help alleviate the edema for Dave, the only other option left was to mechanically pull the edema out of him. This meant dialysis.

For those of you who are not familiar with how dialysis works or the strain it places on the body, let me take a minute to explain it. Also, keep in mind, Dave did not have in stage renal failure, which is usually why people go on dialysis. Because of this, Dave was a candidate to come off dialysis once we stabilized the edema situation. (Hopefully, you're beginning to see how complicated his condition was, and why the path to correcting it was not a simple, straightforward one.) Since the edema from his condition could cause blood infections, all of his dialysis treatments required cleaning his blood versus just pulling fluid. The downside to this is that each time you pull blood to clean and then put it back in the body, you inevitably lose some of the blood. In turn, this drops your hemoglobin levels (hemoglobin is how oxygen is carried throughout your body, which is critical to your body functioning properly.)

So, Dave's levels were checked multiple times a day, and monitored closely during his dialysis treatments. Due to how sick he was when we checked him into the hospital, his hemoglobin level was hovering around 9.0–8.5 (normal is anywhere from 13.5 to 18.0 in a healthy adult), which is low, but not in the danger zone. However, in order to have dialysis, they required a hemoglobin of at least 7.0. Because of how severe his edema was, the nephrologist was being as aggressive as she could to get as much edema out as possible, while ensuring that his body could handle it. Dave was receiving a round of dialysis each day, and typically, we were pulling anywhere from three to four liters of edema out a day! Although he would be exhausted afterwards each day, his body was handling it really well, all things considered. In spite of this, his nephrologist had already discussed with us the probability that Dave would eventually need a blood transfusion, as the road she saw ahead would be months of dialysis.

We told her from the beginning that we wanted to avoid a blood transfusion at all costs because we knew that blood banks did not screen the donated blood for COVID vaccination. As I've already stated, due to our science-based educational backgrounds and faith, Dave and I made the personal choice to avoid the COVID vaccination up until this point, and he didn't want to take any risks that could change that. Especially when there are some all-natural options that could be administered to help raise his red blood cell count without a blood transfusion. Dave's nephrologist understood and initiated the protocol to start Dave on this all-natural method of raising his red blood cell count.

However, as anyone who knows how the life cycle of red blood cells in the body works, it would take anywhere from two to three weeks before the body would receive benefits from this treatment, as that's how long it takes to create new functioning red blood cells. So, it became a balancing act of continuing to push each day to get rid of the edema, while working to maintain a hemoglobin level around 8.0 to keep Dave safe and prevent a blood transfusion. After about eight days of this, and having pulled around forty pounds of weight off of Dave while maintaining a stable hemoglobin level, one morning when blood draws were being done, we noticed that his hemoglobin level had dropped below 7.0. He was hovering around 6.2 or so. This was a dangerous and scary level to say the least. Now, not only was dialysis not an option, but his nephrologist discussed with us the immediate need for a blood transfusion for his long-term prognosis. We were devastated to say the least, and just torn over what to do. I even reached out to the hospital administration seeking alternatives, such as using my own blood for the transfusion. After all, I am O-positive (universal donor), so my blood would be perfect for him.

For the first time during this entire process, I lost my composure out of anger. The hospital told me that their protocol and procedure would not allow me to give my own blood. What? Since when? For years, people have been able to actually go in before a surgery and have their own blood taken to ensure that they received their own blood back during the surgery. Therefore, this answer made no sense to me. Well, apparently within the past few years (since right around the start of the pandemic), the hospital had changed their policy to only use the blood from the Carter blood bank, and this blood bank not only refuses to screen for COVID vaccination, but they also will no longer allow you to donate blood to be used specifically for a relative, someone you know, or even yourself. However, if it was what the hospital deemed an emergency situation, such as he was bleeding out and in immediate danger of dying, then hospital policy would allow me to donate my blood to him. I was furious, and we were beside ourselves trying to decide what was the right thing to do for Dave. Needing specific guidance, Dave and I sat in his hospital room and began praying for God's direction in this.

At the end of the day, we decided to move forward with the transfusion and trust that God would honor our heart's desire to obey Him and protect Dave. The transfusion worked to raise his levels so that he could go back to daily dialysis and follow our original game plan.

Although suffering in this life isn't something we choose for ourselves, how we walk in the midst of the suffering is. Dave walked in a way that taught me so much about the call from the Lord "to suffer well." He didn't allow his feelings during this time to ultimately determine his choices, which he so easily could have done. On any given day during his health battle, but especially during these sixteen days in the hospital, it would have been much easier for Dave to choose the easier route, but he chose to endure the very strenuous and lengthy physical protocol needed for his body to even have the possibility of recovery. Not to mention that the emotional and spiritual toll it took on his human body would naturally stir up anyone's feelings of frustration, anger, resentment, hopelessness, fear, and desperation. However, instead of allowing these feelings to take root inside his heart and mind and poison his soul, he chose to cling to the truth found in the person of Jesus and His Word, and actively place his trust in the outcome of his life to someone bigger than himself and the situation, which in turn brings hope. Because of this, he was able to walk with true joy and peace in the midst of indescribable pain and suffering.

Even when we strive to make choices that we believe are good, right, and aligned with what is best, they don't always lead to our desired outcome. The only choice we are then left with is how we respond to that outcome. The innate human response is to cry about how it's not fair, but as we all know after living for any length of time, life is not fair. Unbeknownst to me, I was about to learn just how unfair life can be.

Before he was released from the hospital sixteen days later, on October 22, 2023, they had pulled an incredible eighty pounds of edema out of him! This even astounded the doctors. We were beginning to see certain kidney numbers coming back up, and the road to recovery was manifesting. Although Dave left the hospital in a wheelchair due to the severe edema that still remained in his legs and feet, we knew that once we were able to remove the remaining edema through continued outpatient dialysis along with physical therapy to get him walking once more, the healing process would speed up. We were hopeful.

# CHAPTER SEVEN

# Letting Go Is Necessary

I look back and realize there were numerous things that the Lord did to prepare my heart for this outcome with Dave, even though I didn't see it at the time, especially in the last thirty-six hours of his life.

The last night in the hospital when Dave went home to be with the Lord, God allowed a beautiful moment to take place. After the critical care doctor had made the decision to intubate Dave because his breathing had become too labored to continue at that rate, Dave's vitals were finally stable and doing well. Friends who were there had gone home, and I asked his brother Ron and sister-in-law PJ to stay with Dave while I went home to take a quick shower and feed the dogs.

When I arrived back at the hospital, Dave was resting (he had been sedated and given pain meds to relax while being intubated), and his blood pressure (BP) and heart rate had remained stable this entire time. However, I noticed as Ron and PJ were getting ready to leave that Dave's BP was beginning to dive down once more. As was the norm in this ICU unit, the nurse immediately saw it and came in the room to increase the BP IV drip and a few other things in order to help stabilize it once more, which it did.

After his brother and sister-in-law had left for the night, I sat down next to Dave's bed to talk to him and tell him why I made the decision to intubate. Dave was adamant that he did not want to be intubated. Neither one of us ever wanted any form of life support to be used on us when the time came. He trusted me to honor his wishes in this, and I was determined to do just that. The only reason I asked the doctor to do otherwise on his behalf was because our friends and his family who were at the hospital, along with the doctors, spent a good amount of time talking to me to make a convincing case for intubation, in spite of my resistance to it. You see, his hospital team fully believed that if they could get his breathing under control, then they would be able to do the tests needed in order to determine if he had acquired a new blood-borne infection or if there was some sort of gut issue taking place, and then move forward with the right course for his healing. But I made it clear that if his status did not show significant improvement within twenty-four hours, I would pull the intubation.

When we checked him into the hospital this time (his second visit), his kidney stats looked better than they had looked in months. The reason we had to come back to the hospital was due to severe pain in his legs, so much so that I couldn't even get him into his wheelchair the day I had to call the ambulance for the second time. The cause for this ended up being blood clots that had developed in his legs, and this is why we were back in the hospital. So, as I was sitting next to the bed this night and talking to Dave, I noticed his BP and heart rate were fluctuating, but stabilized once more by the time I had finished. It was then that I knew Dave was communicating with me in the only way he could. I also realized that he had been waiting for me to get back. Dave could never relax or sleep in the hospital unless he knew I was there to watch and monitor everything that was being done. However, that night, the reason would be more than that.

I had been asking the ICU staff if I could have a patient bed like his so I could sleep next to him, hold his hand, and touch him to let him know I was there. But, because they needed to be able to easily access both sides of his bed, that wasn't possible. So, I pulled the foldout chair that could be made into a bed as close to his bed as I could and laid down for the night. It was probably no more than one hour after I laid down for the night and right as I was starting to fall asleep that I noticed his nurse was back in the room working and monitoring some things. I noticed that his BP was all over the place once more. The nurse was calmly doing the things they had been doing to stabilize his blood pressure, but I noticed that he had to do more things now than a few hours previously. He began giving Dave more platelets, as well as needed to start yet another blood transfusion (this was the third one done during this short hospital stay) as his hemoglobin levels had dropped once more. At this point, the charge nurse came in the room to help, followed soon by more of the nursing staff. I moved over to the corner of the L-shaped room by the door to allow them to work and watched as the tears began to uncontrollably flow down my face. I hadn't slept in more than thirty-six hours at this point, and now I was watching what seemed to be the best chance of getting him back on the road to recovery for his kidneys fading away fast.

As I watched the staff lift the blanket off his legs to do some work/monitoring, what I saw told me all that I needed to know. The respiratory care nurse that was in the room came over to give me a hug and ask if there was anything I needed while she sat with me. I began telling her that "All I want is for him to not be in pain anymore, and to be at peace." I could see that the situation had changed from before I left the hospital to go home, and as I stated, Dave and I had a strong commitment to never be on life support. We believe that God can heal with just one word, and if it was His will for Dave to still be here, He would and could do it no matter what happened in the physical world. (Please don't misunderstand me; I am not opposed to medical life-saving intervention. There are many times when the body needs a "jump start" of sorts in order to start regulating itself properly once more. But there's a difference between that and life support.)

I kept telling the respiratory nurse that all I wanted was to be able to crawl into bed and lay with my husband. I hadn't been able to do this in some time, and I just wanted him to feel and know that I was there. The doctor on call who was working with the nurses overheard me and came over to me and said, "Ma'am, what would you like us to do? We will do whatever you want." I told him, "I have a medical background, and I know what I am seeing. That looks like sepsis, and even if he is able to come off the intubation, it will be so painful. That is no way to live. Just please pull it." The doctor asked, "Pull just the intubation tube or all of it?" I said, "Please, pull it all. I just want him to be able to rest peacefully tonight." I then proceeded to ask, through the tears and barely understandable words I could get out of my mouth, if they would situate him in the bed so that I could crawl into bed with him. I wanted, but more importantly, needed to lay beside my husband. This gracious staff took the time to situate the room for me after pulling all the different tubes and IVs (even put my pillow and blanket beside Dave on his bed for me) so that I could finally lay with my husband.

Once the room was ready, I crawled into bed with Dave, and they left the room. I laid my head on his chest and began telling him how much I loved him, and how proud I was of him. As I was talking, I felt and heard his heart beginning to race, which it hadn't done until now. I knew he heard me and was communicating with me the only way he could. He was telling me that he loved me too. I told him that he was my best friend, better half, and that I didn't know how to do life without him; so, if he could keep fighting and get better, then I wanted him to fight with all that he had. But, if he saw Jesus calling him home, then I wanted him to run towards Him and don't look back. I will be okay. It was at this point that his heart rate began to slow to a steady and peaceful beat for a few more minutes until it stopped. From the time I crawled into the bed until his heart stopped was about ten minutes total.

You see, the connection that Dave and I had allowed us to communicate with one another in a deeper way than mere words ever could have. It was because we had one another's hearts. This is only possible because each of us had the Holy Spirit in us, which was the unifying factor between us. This is so much more powerful and intimate than most of us understand.

During the following weeks after his death, God showed me that He was faithful to the good word He spoke to me about Dave, and He also an-swered a long-time prayer of mine for him. God's good word to me—to trust Him; He had Dave, and He had this—proved to be true. God did; just in a different way than I thought. I also saw him bring to life my favorite scripture verse in Dave's life: "Being confident of this very thing, that He who has begun a good work in you will complete it until the day of Jesus Christ" (Philippians 1:6). I was able to see the completion of what God wanted to do in Dave's life and heart on this Earth. You see, in our hubris, we incorrectly think that the work in us will be completed once we die; however, there is a completion that must take place in us before we die, in order for our spirits to be ready for the kingdom of the Lord and our new bodies. So, you see; how we end the race matters, which is why Paul talks about running the race in such a way as to win. Dave ran his race all the way to the end in such a way as to win, and I am so proud of him! I know he is with the Lord, and I will see him again one day soon.

If you were to ask me to describe how I was feeling then and even now, here is the best way I can put it into words: I would change everything, and at the same time, nothing at all in order for us to have our "happy ever after." It's as if I'm trapped in the in-between of holding tightly to what my heart wanted for Dave/us and letting go, trusting what the Lord ultimately decided is best. In short, a beautiful disaster. Beautiful because I know the Lord is in the midst of all of this, but a disaster nonetheless. So, when I say it's how we respond to circumstances that determine what we get out of this life, it's coming from a place of intimate understanding.

Through this, I have learned that there is a time to fight, and a time to let go. For me, this has been the absolute hardest part of this process for me. The reason for this is because my natural tendency is to oppose change. In many aspects of my life (not all, because there are areas where I want spontaneity), I thrive off structure. So, when this structure/routine is challenged in some significant way, my natural instinct is to fight against it. So, yes; you could say that I can be a bit of a control freak, which is an on-going process of seeking help and guidance from the Lord to change. This doesn't mean that I am advocating for living a life that is "out of control." It's actually the exact opposite. I am suggesting that we choose to surrender the seat of control/power in our lives to the one who is best equipped at controlling everything in the first place: the Lord Jesus.

Why would anyone "in their right mind" ever voluntarily choose to give up control of their own life to anyone or anything else? Well, this is solely guided by and dependent upon what you truly believe about this life and eternity. I, like Dave, believe that there is a creator named Yahweh Elohim—the Lord of Lords, the Great I AM—who spoke everything into existence, from the literal sky above us to our human bodies. Therefore, yes; I believe in frequencies, energy, and vibration (super string theory and harmonic resonance) as they are His creation and are the basis of the sound He used to create this universe in the first place! Following this line of thought down its designed path, I also believe in the law of the natural and spiritual world which states that creation is subordinate to its creator (examples of this can be seen all throughout our natural world). I hope some of you are tracking with me, but hang on, as this is where the first fork in the road shows up in this messy thing called the human existence.

Unless this belief (something that is accepted, considered to be true, or held as an opinion) is allowed to transform into trust in God, it will never manifest the power of God (Yahweh Elohim) in your life. This is why James says, "For as the body without the spirit is dead, so faith without works is dead also" (James 2:26). Choosing to trust God is "the first work" of faith required on our part.

As humans, we can only place our trust in things that we believe are good and have our best interests in mind, right? Let me give you a quick and simple example of this. I *choose* to sit down in a chair because I *believe* it will do the job that it claims to do, which is to keep me off the ground. As a result, I am placing my *trust* in the ability of the chair and not in my ability to keep me from falling. How and why can I do this? Because I believe that the chair's purpose had my best interests in mind when it was created. The same concept is true in our spiritual lives. If you don't truly believe that God is good at His core, which means that you believe His plan for your life is the absolute best thing for you, you will never choose to fully trust Him, as this requires submission and relinquishing of control of your life to Him. In other words, we must go through a metamorphosis, which always begins with death to self. You see, friends, trusting God means trusting His goodness, timing, and hand in our lives, which runs in direct opposition to human nature. That's why it's such a battle for each of us (including myself) because it's a choice between what our flesh desires and what our spirit needs.

For myself and anyone who claims the name of Jesus Christ, we are called to place our full trust in Him alone, as He is the bridge between man and God (John 14:6). You see, it's not enough to just believe in Him, because belief doesn't automatically equate to trust, which is defined as the assured reliance on the character, ability, and strength of someone or something; "You believe there is one God. You do well. Even the demons believe—and tremble!" (James 2:19). You see, whatever we entrust our lives to, ultimately, depends on trust. However, choosing to trust the Lord and relinquish control of our lives requires letting go of our grip over it. If you're like me, this is harder than hell to actually do.

Letting go is scary, but absolutely necessary. However, it is important to note that there is a huge difference between letting go of control and controlling our choices. I am advocating for the first and not the latter here. We will always be in control of the choices we make, as this is the only real control any of us actually have and are given by our Creator in this life. But trying to control every aspect of how this life unfolds is not only counterproductive, but can be detrimental to our well-being. It isn't always negative or harmful things that we must let go of either. It took me a hot minute to understand that this is what was needed in my life right now.

As crazy as this might sound to some of you, after my husband passed away, I found myself in my prayer time asking the Lord to "please take care of Dave for me, and let him know that I loved him." Although there is nothing wrong with desiring these things, in time, the Lord revealed to me that what was actually driving this daily prayer of mine was an unwillingness to let go. You see, this wasn't just a one-time prayer; rather, I found myself daily in tears begging the Lord to take care of Dave. Sounds crazy, right? Especially for someone who would tell you that I believe in the absolute sovereignty of God and that He loves us more than any other human being ever can or ever will. So then, why was I feeling and behaving this way? It took me many months of reflecting on my life, spending time in the Word, and praying to the Lord to finally come to the place of understanding the why behind this.

The hard realization that I came face-to-face with recently was two-fold in nature. Being a full-time caretaker for Dave was the right thing to do and was absolutely needed at the time, but it was also a way in which I tried "to highjack" the situation by seeking control for my desired outcome. My desired outcome to see Dave fully restored physically led me to believe that I needed to be in complete control of the situation, and that doing this would lead to healing. His sickness required this type of care from me for a full year, which demanded all of my time, attention, energy, and commitment. When Dave passed, not only did it leave me stuck underneath the weight and routine of the role of a "failed full-time caretaker," with no idea how to move on from this, but another truth revealed itself: the need to let go of the "what had been" in order to move into the "what will be." If you're anything like me, the question then became "How do I do this?" I have come to learn that whether it is letting go of something harmful or letting go of the good and "what has been," I must acknowledge, embrace, and then let go.

Why do I say this? Well, we can't change what we won't acknowledge. And so, our first steps begin when we admit that we need to *stop* everything, *drop* what we are clinging to, and *deal* with the things occurring in our heart and mind with authenticity. But we can't stop with mere acknowledgment. Once we acknowledge the need, the next step is to embrace it. Let me explain what I mean. The definition of embrace is "to encircle or welcome something/someone." Embracing doesn't mean it has to be permanent; it just means that you accept it as real. Embracing is facing. Embracing is where you feel and deal. Why is this necessary? Because something you embrace, you own, and ownership automatically assumes accountability. How can you let go of that which you do not own? The ironic thing is that we are actually accountable for what we do with our circumstances and feelings whether we choose to own them or not. However, the choice to own it places the feeling/situation directly in our line of sight instead of out of mind. Finally, after all of this, you must choose to let it all go, which requires belief and trust that something great still lies ahead for you.

I share all of this in order to help you understand why I needed to be brought to and through this very hard process of letting go. Dave has finished his race, but I am still running mine. As is true with any race, finishing, much less finishing strong, requires endurance on the part of the runner. It's easy for us to recognize the tools necessary to successfully endure a physical race to its completion (preparation, good hydration, proper footwear, good pacing, etc.), but it becomes a bit more difficult and convoluted for most of us to recognize the same in the spiritual sense.

Although I have discovered that there are a few different things necessary to properly navigate this spiritual race of sorts, one attribute stands out above the rest, as it is the foundation upon which everything else is built—joy, courage, strength, love, and patience. I am referring to peace. More than anything right now, I desperately need peace in my life once more. Not the temporary, situation-dependent feeling of peace that constantly sells itself as the solution for our weary and desperate souls by *only* bringing comfort, which never truly satiates any part of us. But instead, deep down, it leaves us not only still desperate for relief, but actually worse off than when we began. My soul longs for the peace I have known in the past and somehow lost on this journey. The peace that runs much deeper than any feeling ever could as it envelops your heart, soul, and mind in such a way as to become entwined with your literal state of being. The outcome of this type of peace is not rooted in how you feel, nor is it dependent upon your circumstances, as true peace can exist even when everything around you is raging like an F5 tornado. Rather, it controls who you become. It leaves you at peace; it's what the Bible refers to as "the peace of God, which surpasses all understanding, will guard your hearts and minds through Christ Jesus" (Philippians 4:7).

All too often, we mistakenly fall into the trap of believing that peace is the absence of pain and suffering. That is not true because peace is centered around our state of being, not our life circumstances. It is the boat of quiet assurance on the sea of pain and chaos that allows you to safely navigate the storm with joy and the hope of restoration on the other side. Peace is what brings you *through* the storm intact. This peace only comes one way; through the bridge God made for us to get to Him. We need a bridge to get to God because a chasm exists between this Holy God and sinful humanity. But as humans, we try to create "work arounds" for the things we desire in our lives, including peace. How we can honestly expect to receive true peace by bypassing *The Prince of Peace?* His name is Jesus Christ, and He is the bridge: "For unto us a Child is born, Unto us a Son is given; And the government will be upon His shoulder. And His name will be called Wonderful, Counselor, Mighty God, Everlasting Father, Prince of Peace" (Isaiah 9:6). Only the author of such peace is able to offer it to others. I needed to let go and trust in God's goodness for me and His plan for my life, which will always necessitate full submission of control over my life to Jesus. In other words, death to self. Because He not only has the absolute best planned for me, but He also knows the end from the beginning. I had to come to the end of myself because God begins where we end.

Being able to finally let go is a process whose timeline is different, yet necessary for each of us. You will find that grief is a large part of this process, and it can be a fickle lady to say the least.

# CHAPTER EIGHT

# Grief Is a Funny Thing

To everything there is a season, a time for every-
thing under heaven:
A time to be born,
And a time to die;
A time to plant,
And a time to pluck what is planted;
A time to kill,
And a time to heal;
A time to break down,
And a time to build up;
A time to weep,
And a time to laugh;
A time to mourn,
And a time to dance;
A time to cast away stones,
And a time to gather stones;
A time to embrace,
And a time to refrain from embracing;
A time to gain,
And a time to lose;
A time to keep,
And a time to throw away;
A time to tear,

And a time to sew;
And a time to keep silence,
And a time to speak;
A time to love,
And a time to hate;
A time of war,
And a time of peace.

These words were not coined by a well-known musician or song writer, but rather came from the wisest man to ever live: King Solomon. You will find these words in Ecclesiastes 3:1–8. They came to mind as I began writing this chapter.

It has been thirteen months since I delivered the eulogy at Dave's funeral. Even though we can and should expect to walk through grief whenever we suffer loss or intense pain of any kind, its' timing can be different for everyone. Often, it hits you when you least expect it. At least, this has been my experience.

At the same time that my late husband's condition reached a point where he could no longer work (early 2023), my older brother, Tim, began to have some on-going GI issues. Due to his mental and physical handicaps, he had been on numerous medications his entire life. Whether all of these were necessary or not was an on-going debate that my mom and I had with one another. The side effects of many of these medications were just unbelievable, and made certain daily activities hard for him at times. In my opinion, the risks did not outweigh the reward. Needless to say, my mom's first reaction to any medical imbalance/issue with herself or Tim was always to seek out the "fastest fix" possible versus working towards a long-term solution for true healing. I have come to understand over the years that this didn't come from a place of malicious intent or because she didn't love him; she loved Tim as much as she was able to know and show love.

Along with these medical choices, fear drove my mom's decision-making process in almost all aspects of her life, especially when it came to my brother. Tim has always been a main focal point of her life, as he needed so much attention and care, especially when he was younger. But now, he had become her whole life. Don't get me wrong; I am not saying there is anything wrong with loving your kids and family with all of your heart to the point of being willing to sacrifice everything for them. I believe that is exactly what unconditional love does. However, there is a difference between being confident in who you were created to be as a human so that you can unconditionally love others versus finding your identity and worth in another human being. The second will never allow you to authentically love others unconditionally. This was all my mom knew; she found her identity in being a mom—mainly Tim's mom. Because of this, she was willing to follow the advice any doctor gave her in a misplaced hope that the recommended protocol would "fix" his situation. With that said, I found that many times, the solutions presented by his various doctors created more problems than solutions. Tim had been having severe IBS symptoms that would make him miserable for weeks on end, as well as make it hard to take him out in public for anything during this time. Not to mention that my mom struggled with the lack of a desire to cook most days, as well as using good judgement when it came to her eating habits.

All of this to say that there were multiple compounding things that led to Tim's health deteriorating to the point that in May 2024 (five months after Dave passed), I was forced to take over full-time care and custody of my brother. Mind you, this was done against my mother's will, as she had always been his guardian and had no intention of ever giving that up to anyone else. Without going into all the details behind this story (the details are ugly and personal), it was after I found my brother in a trauma room at the local ER in the middle of the night by himself with no pants and a filthy shirt looking scared and confused, while my mom was lying in a different ER room with the TV on and sleeping because she had checked herself into the hospital as a patient when she checked in Tim, that I took him home with me for good. Because of this, I now found myself as a full-time caregiver once more for someone with a serious medical condition.

Around the time of this ER incident, we discovered that Tim had colorectal cancer, and there was a huge mass that had developed which was causing all of his GI issues. This required a loop colostomy procedure in order to clear out the blockage and so we could determine the steps forward for healing and a full recovery with his oncologist. Due to the size of the mass, surgery was not an option, for now. So, I worked hand in hand with his oncologist and GI doctors to find the best, safest, and most effective protocol for Tim, which was a full-time job for me. Tim lived with me and fought hard to recover, but for reasons I do not understand, God's plan for him was different. He passed away on August 17, 2024 (eight months and two days after I lost Dave). I will always cherish these months with Tim in my care, as it created the opportunity for the first time in our lives to be able to share some very sweet moments. As I've said many times previously, caring in this capacity for Dave and Tim was the greatest privilege of my life, and I would do it all over again without hesitation. These were two of the three most important men in my life, whom I loved very much. However, this type of care drains you in every possible way, and the struggles and hits just wouldn't seem to let up for me.

Because my mom was completely heartbroken and relied on income from being my brother's caretaker to support all of her monthly expenses, following his death, she could no longer live on her own. With no money or other options available to her, in October 2024, I moved my mom in with me. As you might suspect, this was not "an ideal" situation due to the strained relationship my mother and I have always had. She had a way of making everyday life just plain hard for everyone around her, but especially for me. In spite of that, she was my mom. Without this living arrangement as an option, she would have been on the streets. I couldn't allow that to happen. Having her in my home was a struggle to say the least. She needed a walker to get around due to a deteriorating knee and chronic back pain. Not to mention, she was working to control her type 2 diabetes.

I always struggled to find the balance between drawing a line in the sand that I would not allow her to cross and showing grace when it came to my mom. You see, after we lost my dad, she made Tim her reason to live. So, from her vantage point, now that Tim was gone, she no longer had a reason to live.

It was somewhere around the first few days in January of this year (2025) when, for the first of two different times, my mom woke up in a completely altered state that left her unable to speak coherently or move properly on her own. After a few hours and when she was able to communicate clearly, I confronted her about the pills I had found. It was clear that her long-time addiction to pain and sleeping pills—that I helped her overcome eight years ago—had made a comeback. At first, she denied that she had taken anything the previous night. However, the body doesn't lie. So, I knew otherwise, and she eventually admitted as much. Then, the same thing happened a mere seven days later. An intense discussion followed the second instance. Her response to me regarding our discussion about how something had to change was dismissed with excuses and she chose to only focus on her pain. It was as if, all of a sudden, I had hit a brick wall. I had to sit down, literally. I couldn't do anymore. I was completely spent emotionally, mentally, physically, and spiritually at this point.

Here is the best way to describe how I was feeling in this moment—and had been for a while. I was spent, and my heart had become burdened from the energy it took just to keep breathing most days. I knew that I needed to redirect the gaze of my heart upward towards the only one who I truly believed could redeem a heart with authentic peace and rest, but I was literally too weak to do it. The overwhelming heaviness of the world around me had replaced the hope and peace which once made its home in my heart and mind, not to mention that this train of pain wasn't slowing down, much less coming to a stop anytime in the foreseeable future. Although I have always cherished my intimate time in the Word and prayer, as well as have always been a tenacious fighter in life, my prayers felt as if they were falling on deaf ears, and I had literally lost my will to fight. I was completely overwhelmed and felt totally alone. I had reached a point where I just couldn't keep going.

The reason I am sharing all of this with you is because I believe that many of you can relate to how I was feeling, and, as odd as it sounds, this was what it took to force me to work through the remaining unresolved grief I didn't yet realize existed. The truth is that each of us have different coping mechanisms to help us get through hard times in life. For me, staying as busy as possible with other important things in my daily routine has always been my mechanism of choice. However, I couldn't see this because my daily routine had received "an unrequested upgrade" with the role of full-time caretaker. The necessity and importance of this role made it much easier for me to hide behind the daily demands of what needed to be done for others, and therefore, never make the time to be honest with myself concerning what I wasn't acknowledging in my own heart and life. The saying "Time heals all wounds" is a lie, friends. It's not time that heals anything; it's what is done in that time that either leads to healing or further destruction. Let me state this caveat; I am not saying that staying busy is a bad thing in and of itself. Getting back to your everyday normal routine can be healthy during difficult times. However, what isn't healthy is using your routine as a way to avoid dealing with the reality of your emotional and spiritual state because of your trauma. It wasn't until now that I realized this is exactly what I had been doing. For me, my daily routine only somewhat resembled "normal" because I kept getting hit with struggle after struggle; none of which were my choosing and all of which made the waters of daily life even murkier. So, choosing to focus on other people's issues while avoiding the lingering unresolved issues in my own heart and soul was the path of least resistance for me because they were just too hard to face.

You know, the grief process is a funny thing. Just when you think that you are working through it well and getting closer to being "whole" once more, something happens that triggers you in a way to help you realize some deeply rooted, unresolved issues and lingering pain. This is what happened to me. As a naturally creative personality and soul, I tend to find comfort, healing, and challenge in being able to authentically feel and communicate, whether it's via a character in an impactful story brought to life on screen through acting, or lending a listening ear while having a conversation, or by giving what's inside a voice through the written word. And what has been the toughest part of all of this for me is the fact that no one in my immediate reality can relate to what I have been experiencing. Not that there aren't people in my life who can't relate to aspects of my experience, because there are. There just isn't another person I know who can relate to the amount, timeline, and degree of the loss and pain I have been experiencing. Please hear me when I say that this makes my heart glad, as I would never want anyone to experience what I have over the past three years. But, this truth has left me feeling very alone, and as if I didn't have an outlet though which to express myself and therefore, truly grieve.

My close friends will tell you that I love to sleep (not that I sleep all the time, but when it is time to sleep, I do so with no problems). However, during this difficult season of my life, my sleep was affected for the first time. For about five days straight, it was good if I got two hours of sleep each night, and I had no desire to sleep during the day either. Because of this, I found myself looking for a way to distract and even quiet my mind that wouldn't stop racing in the middle of the night. Have you ever been in the place where you couldn't shut off your thoughts? Where they are like a runaway train with no station in sight? This was where I found myself. Although I don't watch much TV at all, I found myself turning on the TV in the middle of the night as a means to try and stop my racing thoughts. I know you might think it is strange for someone in the entertainment industry to not watch much in the way of TV or film, but most of my days are busy and filled with living life, so I don't have time or really the desire to search out things to watch. However, I do have my guilty pleasures that I will watch when I can.

From the time I moved my mom into my house with me, I was on the search for a few different family-friendly, or at least "more wholesome," shows for her to watch. That was how she passed most of her days and had for years. Thanks to modern-day streaming services, she was able to watch a few different shows in their entirety. It was during this time that I found what seemed to be a wholesome family show with sixteen seasons on Amazon Prime for her to watch. She quickly became hooked on the show. So much so that many times, I would discover she had been up all night watching it. So, out of curiosity and the need to quiet my thoughts during this time when I couldn't sleep, I decided to start watching the show myself. Even though my mom and I have very different tastes in most things, often including entertainment, to my surprise, I found myself drawn to the show as well. However, the reason for me was very different and unexpected. You see, the love story that played out between the two main characters was eerie yet comforting in how similar it was to my and Dave's story. So, watching this unfold forced me to re-experience many aspects of our relationship that I had forgotten, or maybe even chose to overlook. I came to find this very therapeutic, as it became an outlet for me to feel and deal in a way I hadn't up to that point. It is also the time when I began writing this book as an outlet to express what I was feeling and experiencing for the first time.

One of the greatest reminders and insight that the Spirit had been speaking to me during this time was that there is a difference between the voice of guilt and the voice of conviction. One is healthy and for your good, while the other is harmful and meant for your destruction. Guilt tells you that you have no intrinsic value, which leads to depression, anxiety, feelings of worthlessness, paranoia, and, ultimately, bondage. Its source is the enemy of our souls. Guilt is meant for your condemnation. Whereas conviction, on the other hand, is never meant to question your value as a creation of God, rather, it is meant to lovingly shine light on the truth of your current state in a way that compels you to honestly assess and mourn your shortcomings/failures. When allowed to properly do its job, conviction leads to joy, hope, and freedom. Its source is the creator of life. Conviction is meant for your restoration. Deciphering between the two is key. It has become clear to me that, during the past thirteen months, I have been allowing the voice of guilt to lead me, not only with certain aspects of my relationship with Dave, but with my mom as well.

Another element that contributed to this period of intense loss was what I can only describe as a wholesale purging process in my life. It wasn't just a purging of a few things or areas, but it felt like an all-out fire sale that was initiated against my will—at least in most areas of my life. Long before 2019, we had been purging unhealthy things from our lives, specifically in the area of our health. You could say that I was "red pilled" concerning the highjacking of the medical system years ago while I was still in college. However, in 2019, the Lord began revealing so many other things where we needed to take a "deeper look," and we did. This choice to search for truth, wherever it may lie, led to the need to purge even more things from our lives. As hard as it was, this included placing distance and even cutting ties altogether from specific relationships in our lives. It was and is not an easy thing to do. Purging isn't easy because it requires that you go through a refining process, and this process entails intensity, heat, and pressure in order to be done properly. When you think about it, it's very similar to the refining process for gold. In order for gold to be made pure, it has to go through an intense and repetitious refining process. It's not a one-time thing. Intense heat and pressure is used in a repeated process until all the impurities have melted away and the only product you are left with is pure gold. This is exactly what the Lord uses the purging process for in our lives. It's meant to get rid of the things that aren't the best for you in order to make room for the things that are, and at times, to make room for the "what's next" in your story. This can and usually is hard for our hearts to understand and/or accept because we can so easily get lost in the pain of the process. This was what happened to me.

It was becoming clear to me that I was holding onto guilt in some areas like a dog with a bone; unwilling to let go, and more importantly, unaware that guilt was driving this behavior. The strange thing is that guilt can grip us and keep us from letting go of things (the bondage I referred to earlier), not only of unhealthy patterns, but also of healthy and good things. Let me share with you two things (one "unhealthy/bad" and one "healthy/good") that became apparent in my life during this time of sitting still and waiting on God to meet me in my pain and exhaustion.

Watching this show and being able to relate to the dysfunctional family relationships that one of the main characters had with his parents made me take a deeper and honest look into my relationship with my mom. I, once again, had to acknowledge how that relationship impacted my life and dictated many decisions over the years. Dave and I never had kids, not because we didn't want them or couldn't have them, but mainly because, from the beginning of our marriage, we wanted to spend the time with one another to solidify our relationship before adding kids to the mix. We both had seen in our families what happens when couples have kids immediately and make them the center of their existence: The marriage relationship takes a back seat and suffers, quite often to the point where the relationship between the spouses is practically nonexistent. We didn't want this to happen to us. Our initial plan was to wait five years, and then reassess. But five years became five more years, and so on. However, what wasn't apparent to me for most of my adult life was the role my relationship with my mom played in this decision for me. The reality for me was that after my father passed away when I was very young, I became "the parent" in my home virtually overnight. This was because my mom chose to "check out of life" due to her subsequent depression. I am not condemning her for this, just stating the facts behind why it happened. This remained the case to a large extent for the rest of her life. Not only did I manage high school and put myself through college on my own, but I spent all my life bailing my mom out of one disastrous situation after another. I always told myself that I only did this for my brother's sake, and that if my brother wasn't in the picture, I would have cut her off a long time ago.

This period of grieving and reflection revealed a deeper truth that I hadn't ever wanted to admit, which was that I did all of this, and am still doing this even though Tim has passed, because I feel responsible for ensuring my mom is healthy, and always have. When this truth hit me, I immediately knew in my mind that this wasn't healthy, good, or even possible. So, then why was I allowing this feeling/thought process to guide and control my actions? The answer wasn't complicated to admit; rather, just harder than hell to admit. I felt guilty, and continue to feel guilty, about her situation in life. Was this because I hadn't been there for her throughout her life, or because I did things that caused her to struggle or be where she was? No. Now, I am not saying that I was the perfect daughter who never made any mistakes. First, that's not possible, but more importantly, it's not about being perfect. Mistakes in relationships can and will be made. That's part of the human experience. So, the question became "Then, why do I feel guilty?" Watching the details of a similar dysfunctional parent-child relationship play out in this show and through time spent in prayer showed me that the guilt

117

I was feeling came from a place of feeling the need to control my mom. Like I said previously, I have always struggled with trying to control all aspects of my life. Because I loved her and wanted the best for her, I convinced myself that it was my responsibility to do whatever it took to keep her from hurting herself and to get her to choose the right path in life. But the truth is, this was not my responsibility; it was always hers. It was after that intense discussion about her addiction to sleeping pills that I knew I had come to the end of the road of trying to make her change. It became clear that I had to get off this merry-go-round of chaos, and I had to be the one to initiate the change.

Deep down, I have always thought to myself "How could I trust someone so unstable with my children, even though I would want nothing more than for them to know their grandma?" But, I also feared being a mom with young kids and finding myself needing to bail my mom out of a disastrous situation without the ability to do so. After all, I was the only family she had left; if I didn't help her, who would? In a strange way, I viewed myself as already having a child who needed me. This is how the voice of guilt works on us. It speaks in a way that will lead you down a path of condemnation and scarcity in life, instead of health and abundance. It is never based in truth, but lies. As freeing as it was to come to grips with this and finally let go of it, I found that there was a harder and less obvious thing that I needed to face as well.

It's easy to accept that we need to let go of what we view as "harmful" behaviors/mentalities, but it becomes harder to let go of things we see as being "for our good." Something I have always said over my years of marriage to Dave was

"If anything ever happens to you, I am not getting married again. I had this one, and I'm good." I have even told others this very thing. This has been my mantra since Dave passed. I have told myself and others that I had something great, and now it's gone. So, moving forward, I am good to be by myself. In full transparency, I truly believed this was the best thing for me; at least this is what I had convinced myself of. It wasn't until now, with this time to allow myself to reflect, feel, and deal, that I was able to hear the voice of conviction over the voice of guilt speaking to me in this. Something the Spirit spoke very clearly to me was this, "How can you say you are open and good with whatever I determine is next for you when you have already determined what isn't next?" I knew that the Lord was directly speaking to me about digging in my heels on not finding a partner again in life. This one cut deep, and it has taken me a hot minute to understand the why behind this.

As you have heard me express multiple times in this book, my personality and nature are rooted in establishing intimate connections with others. This is where my true passion in life lies and where I find meaning and joy. Therefore, the idea that I was created to walk this life alone is an oxymoron. However, the odd thing about me is my somewhat dichotomous personality. Although I absolutely love deep and meaningful relationships with others, I also need my "alone time"; I always have. Being around people 24/7 is a no-go for my sanity (can I get an amen from anyone on this?), but that doesn't mean that it is good for me to go it alone either. Deep down, I have always known this to be true, and if I'm being completely honest, I miss having a best friend and partner with whom I can walk this life. So, then why had I dug my heels in on going it alone, or at least, why not be open to the possibility of finding a best friend and true love once more?

I have come to realize that this was not only a way I was protecting my heart from the potential pain of not being desirable to someone else, but mainly, it was rooted in a lie coming from guilt. When I was willing to get brutally honest with myself, I saw a real fear that existed. I had been deathly afraid that "moving on" with someone else would be the equivalent of forgetting and diminishing everything I had with Dave. I just didn't understand how I could ever fully love again when I had already given my whole heart to someone else. He had my heart, and I had his. So, the thought of a new relationship just didn't seem right to me.

But the truth is that the Lord created us for more than we can fathom with our human minds. After all, we are His craftsmanship, created for something amazing and beautiful. If we can believe that He created this world and us, then why would we ever think that a thoughtful and loving Creator would have anything less than the absolute best in store for us? He created us for companionship with Him and others. It took a lot of time and revelation from the Lord in this to allow the eyes of my heart to see and understand the mysterious concept that God works in our hearts and lives for our good, even when we don't see it. I had to tune my ears and heart once more to the voice of truth. Truth will always call us to step out of our comfort zone into the realm of the unknown because that's where Jesus reigns: on the raging sea of uncertainty—where He stands calmly, holding out his hand in the midst of the storm.

Although the waves around you constantly call out to you and repeatedly tell you that you'll never win, you must focus with intentionality to hear his voice over all the other "white noise." His voice sings a different song over you, which says, "Do not be afraid. This is for my glory and for your good. There is a purpose and plan in your pain. Follow me, and I will show you the rest of the story." I am convinced He is not done writing my story, and the best is yet to come!

# Trust the Master Painter

Although it drove me crazy more often than not, my late husband's all-time favorite word was *why*. This started early in life for Dave. It wasn't because he wanted to be difficult (at least not most of the time) or because he didn't have the intelligence to understand most things. Instead, it came from an innate curiosity and drive to dig deeper and understand what made things the way they were. This was the case in all aspects of life for Dave. Anyone who has taken a personality quiz or knows about the Enneagram will find this familiar. Dave was what many people would label a "C" on the personality quiz and six wing five on the Enneagram. Sixes are loyal and productive, logical thinkers who always want to organize their thoughts and actions around what will be the most advantageous for the common good. They also tend to be perfectionists. Because of this, Dave needed to know as much information as possible, and would keep going until he got all the answers he needed; hence the question *why*.

However, I would like to state something clearly here ... although there is a great deal of truth in these particular characteristics of Dave's personality and knowing this can shine some light as to why we have the inclinations that we do, neither he nor I chose to lean into any "categorizing system" such as these for understanding who we were created to be. Here's why: We believed that he is a son of the King, and I am a daughter of the King, this means that our identity is found in Jesus alone. I merely mentioned both of these as a point of reference to help explain his personality in a more tangible way.

With that said, because of his innately inquisitive nature, he helped balance me, as this is not the main aspect of my personality at all. As such, it has never been my first instinct to ask why something happened of God when hard times come. Mainly because I learned at an early age, that more often than not, we will never know the why behind these things this side of eternity. For me, all this question does is leave you in a constant state of turmoil and unable to heal and move forward in life. But this doesn't mean that why should never be asked. There are some situations when understanding the why behind it is necessary to make the changes needed to prevent the same thing from happening in the future. What I am specifically addressing here are the circumstances in life that happen to us with no apparent reason. With that said, there is a how question that I have learned to ask that is always healthy and necessary. It is the question that I had to ask myself now: "How do I move forward in this new reality? What now, God?" I couldn't see how it was possible to restore my heart to completeness so that I could potentially experience a new opportunity for a deep and intimate relationship once more. Although I don't understand the specifics behind how the Lord does this in our lives, I can confidently tell you that He can and does do this for us when we allow Him. With that said, it is a partnership with the Lord. You see, we have a part to play in this. We must choose to allow Him to work on our hearts and be willing to take the brave and difficult steps necessary to step out into the realm of the unknown where faith abides, even when the road ahead is unclear and scary. We must take the first step.

For me, that road is scary because it isn't merely a new or the next chapter in my life; it's an entirely new story that needs to be written. My mom unexpectedly passed away on Valentine's Day this year (February 2025), literally one week after I began writing this book. Within a fourteen-month time span, I had lost all of my remaining family. It looks like my time of breaking down wasn't over yet. This hit me as I was sitting in the funeral home for my mom's public viewing the night before her burial. As her tribute video was playing, I felt as if the wind had been knocked out of me when one of the pictures popped up on the screen. It was a wedding photo of Dave and I with my mom and brother. When I looked at it, it hit me that I was the only person still alive in that picture. The rest of my family was gone now. All of a sudden, thoughts of being broken, a loser with no family that no one else will ever desire, and more started to flood my thoughts. Almost as fast as those thoughts and lies started racing through my mind, I began to hear the Spirit speak reminders of truth to me.

I was reminded that our life is the Lord's canvas on which He paints a beautiful masterpiece. We aren't in control of the brush strokes; He is. And I trust Him. It was this that allowed me to acknowledge these thoughts/feelings as lies, and begin to let go of what was so that I could move with faith into what will be. With the knowledge and understanding that this is not forgetting nor diminishing those relationships, but rather allowing the Lord to finish painting my masterpiece, which is not yet complete. Dave's was completed; mine is still a work in progress. So, while I will forever be grateful for the time, love, and lessons I received from my beautiful relationship with Dave and my family with the knowledge that they will always be a part of me, for the first time, I am excited and ready to discover what life holds next.

Although we may not always be able to control our circumstances, the one thing we can always control is our perspective of our circumstances. After all, it's ultimately our perspective that determines direction in life, and both are a choice. Why go backwards when the Lord has set a new path forward for you?

I realize that many of you reading this either don't believe in or have a hard time believing in God for various reasons. I respect and even sympathize with that, especially if you have been dealt a crap hand in life. It may seem impossible to believe or even conceive of how the love and hope that I have written about is possible for you, but truth and my experience tell me it is. Our time together has been about sharing my journey to healing and hope, neither of which could have happened without the most amazing relationship in my life: my relationship with the Lord. The most unbelievable thing to me about the Lord is that He desires and holds out this same offer for an intimate relationship to each of us. Therefore, my encouragement to you is to forget all the lies and half-truths that religion and the world have told you about God. Instead, take Him at His word. His Word clearly says that He loves you unconditionally with an everlasting love, so much so, that He sacrificed everything in order to have an intimate relationship with me and you!

Many times over the years, but even more recently, when people hear me talk about the Spirit of God in me speaking to me, they will ask me "What does this feel like? Can you describe it to me? How do I know if it's the Spirit speaking or not?" Here's my answer to this. More often than not, I hear it as a still, small voice from within. Beyond that, this experience is hard to put into words, as it is the supernatural playing out in the natural. With that said, here is my best attempt at giving words to something that words will never be able to fully describe.

> It's more than a feeling. It's a presence that brings peace and an overwhelming, inexplicable understanding that you are safe, held, and most importantly, intimately known and loved. It's not fleeting like feelings. It's your constant companion, so you are never alone. It brings your heart, mind, and body into homeostasis. There is nothing more powerful in the human experience than this. Who doesn't want to be seen and intimately loved and known? This is a desire that unites us as humans.

So, how do you move past pain into a hopeful future? Let me share two last things with you that I believe will help with this. The first thing that worked for me, and I am confident will work for all of you, is this: Learn to make space for grace, not only for others, but for yourself as well. What do I mean by this? Notice I said to make space for grace because it is something that we need to be given. Look at the definition of the word grace with me for a moment, and you will understand why I say this.

*Grace*: unmerited divine assistance given to humans for their regeneration or sanctification; favor.

As I've said, you can't give what you've never received. It's easy to blame and retain anger or animosity towards things when we are wrongfully or unintentionally hurt by them, especially people. However, when we choose to make space for the Lord to give us the grace for the situation, the restoration of our hearts and lives can happen. I realize that this can feel impossible for some due to the source of your pain and hurt. Unfortunately, there are some incredibly vile and unbelievable atrocities that are imposed on people in this world. I can't even begin to imagine the immense amount of pain and destruction this brings into the life of those who suffer this. So, please hear me when I say, this word is not meant to marginalize your experience in any way. Instead, it is meant to shine light onto the way out of this darkness that has gripped your heart and soul. Making space for grace for those who have hurt and offended us is for our healing and restoration, not theirs. I had to do this very thing myself. It is not only important that we make space for this with others, but with ourselves as well. This might be the hardest one of the two to do; at least it is for me. Allow yourself to receive the grace being freely offered to you. This is how you shed the blame, feelings of guilt, and regret that can eat us alive after experiencing suffering and loss. It's also the path to restoration and healing for your heart, soul, and mind.

The key to receiving grace and beginning the restoration process is the glue that holds all of this together: faith. Not blind faith in just anything, but rather, an unbridled faith in the belief that you were fearfully and wonderfully made by a God who would move the mountains to know you and be known by you because He loves you. This brand of faith distributes hope that never ends, even when the world is crashing down around you, and allows broken hearts to become brand new.

Ultimately, it's not about perfection; it's about understanding that it's okay to be authentically broken in this unbelievably broken world, as that is the canvas necessary to bring to life an authentically beautiful masterpiece. The art of kintsugi powerfully displays this like nothing else I know. I recently came across a picture and description of kintsugi art, and it profoundly resonated with my soul because this type of Japanese art is deeply symbolic. Kintsugi takes a creation of pottery that has been broken into many pieces and repairs it with gold strands that seal the pieces back together. Not only does this leave the pottery stronger than it was previously, but the gold strands seen throughout add layers of depth to the piece that would not have existed otherwise, which gives it a true beauty and character that its "perfect state" never could. In other words, its strength is made perfect through its weak spots. You see, the approach of this art is to highlight the imperfections, rather than hiding them. Due to the technical nature of this craft and because they appreciate the frail condition of the pottery as well as respect what it once was, only a master kintsugi artist can achieve this. The same is true with us, friends. In the hands of the master painter, what seems like an ugly broken clay jar of a life that has been smashed into a thousand pieces can be lovingly crafted into an amazing work of art that functions as a brand new creation. This is the concept behind the depiction on the cover of this book, as well as what has been unfolding in my life.

God is more than capable of taking the broken pieces of your life and creating a masterpiece more beautiful than you could ever imagine. My prayer for you and everyone who reads this is that out of all the voices calling out to your heart and mind, you will choose to listen and believe the voice of truth, and that you will feel the love that I am imparting to you as I say once more ... you are not alone. Your story and your life matter to God and to me.

# A Letter to Young Widows

All of a sudden finding yourself a widow definitely counts as "the unexpected." As a matter of fact, the very idea that I was now a widow never even crossed my mind until the first time I heard someone refer to me as one. I literally hated it every time I heard that title for a long time. It felt as if I was being "branded and tagged" (makes me think of the book *The Scarlet Letter*), a title that I was too young to bear, much less ever wanted. Not to mention, wearing this "letter of sorts" places you in what feels like a forgotten class in our society. This is at the heart of the many battles that I would have to learn how to navigate in this new reality that had been thrust upon me. I have a feeling that many of you in a similar situation can relate all too well.

Therefore, I wanted to take this time to speak a word of encouragement, strength, peace, and blessing into and over each of you, as young widows have a very tender place in my heart. There are so many lessons that the Lord has taught me and is still teaching me through this process, which means there's no way I could possibly share them all in this book. Instead, I want to share some of the biggest things that come to mind as I think about the specific, strenuous challenges that young widows, like myself, will face.

First, unless they are a young widow themselves, the truth is that most people do not have any idea of your circumstance because they cannot understand what it's like to be you. As humans, we cannot relate to that which have not walked through ourselves; this is just the reality of human nature. Because of this, most people's attempts to help you or be there for you are not only usually confined to the time period immediately following the loss of your spouse (up to about three months after they pass, if you're fortunate), and more often than not, don't meet the most pressing needs in your current reality, but they also are completely unaware of the very unique situation of a young widow. At least, this has been the case for me. Whether it's in the area of your now diminished or altogether lost income, prescient physical labor needs in or around the home, your newfound reality of no longer knowing where you fit in your social circle/society as you are no longer a couple, or any of the many other issues that are part of this new reality, you will find that available resources which offer support from the government, society at large, or even the church are virtually nonexistent. This is especially true if you never had children and your spouse was not in the US military.

I don't know about you, but for me, early on in this journey, whenever I would hear a woman or man in their "golden years" in life say to me that they too are a widow, and know what I am going through because they lost their spouse/best friend of fifty or more years, for the longest time, it would just infuriate me on the inside. Even though this still causes me to cringe when I hear it, the intense anger no longer boils up within me because I realize that their intention is not to minimize my loss or impose any more hurt upon my heart, which is exactly what this felt like. However, the sheer ignorance and lack of understanding in such a sentiment is what I still find unfathomable and heartbreaking at the same time. Although I would never want to diminish the pain from a loss of any kind, especially that of a spouse, as losing a spouse/lifelong companion after decades together brings its own type of pain, the fact remains it is not the same as losing a spouse/best friend unexpectedly early into or only midway through your life together. This is because death is expected at some point in this life, usually our later years. All of this to say, you are now part of a club that you never desired to join, and one in which only the small handful of other members will ever truly understand you. Knowing this doesn't diminish or change this unfortunate behavior from others, but it does allow you the grace that is needed in order to deal with it in a way that doesn't destroy your spirit or theirs.

Second, there's something unique that happens in traumatic experiences that forces you to deal with yourself in a way that nothing else can. So, you will probably experience a time of personal growth that unexpectedly results in the loss of some relationships in your life. As humans, our natural instinct is to perceive loss of any kind as a negative or harmful thing. However, this is not always the case, especially when it is the result of an intentional purging process being implemented. Pain or loss that wounds a soul at the deepest levels (such as the death of a spouse), for one reason or another, results in all of the relationships in your life being run through a filter of sorts. Part of the reason for this is the new lens through which you now view life, but the other reason for this is because it's always the toughest challenges in life that test and reveal the true character of people. I have seen this manifest with three different outcomes during this journey for me. Certain authentic friendships have been sweetened and deepened throughout this journey. These are found in those friends and loved ones who are willing to jump into the muck and mire of this experience to walk it out with you every step of the way. There is nothing more beautiful and soul touching than having the privilege of being on one end of such a relationship. Then, there have been the people with whom I have had to sever ties. For me, these have been the most numerous, as well as the hardest to accept. By sever ties, I don't mean completely cut off all interaction and communication, at least not with the majority of those in this category, but some. What I mean is that I had to remove these people from my inner circle of those with whom I walk daily life because it became clear that we possess two different spirits and are walking two very different paths in this life.

The most unexpected category of relationships that changed for me was in the relationships with other couples Dave and I had in our lives. This category is tough to navigate because it's much more vague than the other two, and the need for change in these relationships only exists because of your new circumstance in life. This has been especially true for the relationships with couples who were in my life because of an existing relationship Dave had with the husband. Although undesired on your part, a shift in the dynamics of the relationship is necessary out of respect for the relationship between the two people who make up that couple, as well as out of respect for you own character and integrity. This is not impossible to navigate (as the Lord has shown me how to do this with one such couple whose husband was one of Dave's close friends, and he has been a godsend of protection and provision in areas where I need a man's skill and knowledge). However, you will find that if you can push through the awkwardness for both sides and focus on the love that existed and bonded all of you in the first place, you will find your way into a new and in some ways, more fulfilling relationship on the other side.

Third, you'll never stop loving or missing your deceased spouse/and or relationship, and that is okay. Contrary to what the most popular quotes and many people say, healing is not about forgetting, leaving behind, or even moving past the person or relationship that was lost. Doing any of those requires you to lose yourself, because in marriage, two become one, which is by design. You will find, at least this has been true for me, the problem that occurs when you fall into any of these false mindsets is that you have a distorted understanding of the nature of the healing process, which in turn, leads to the halting of the healing process in your life. Now, you become stuck in the pain. So, if you can approach the healing process with the proper mindset and expectations, it will allow you to move through it in a smoother, more direct path and timeline than what would otherwise be possible. Also, don't rush the healing process, like I have tried to do so many times since all of this craziness in my life began with Dave's passing. I do this out of a desperate desire to finally be on the other side of all of it where my new story gets to rule the day. There is nothing wrong with this desire. But true healing is a process that must run its course through to completion, in order for you to be the best you for yourself, others, and this world. This timeline is very specific to the individual, and therefore, different for each of us.

Fourth, the you today is different than the you who got married or started dating all those years ago. So, it's more than okay if your life moving forward looks totally different. This is actually an extension of what we just discussed and piggybacks off that concept. When you met your former spouse, you were a different person, at a different place in life (financially, emotionally, possibly professionally, maybe even geographically, etc.) with different needs than you have now. I am so appreciative of the friend who spoke this truth to me during my journey. I hadn't ever thought about this prior to Virginia saying it, but it's so true. We so easily forget that our life prior to our spouse was shaped and marked by the choices, actions, and experiences we had as a single individual. Once we joined ourself with another human being in marriage/partnership, all of our choices, actions, and experiences encompassed the *we* instead of merely the *me*. Therefore, your life now bears the markings and results of this, which means you can never go back to the you from before. This is not a bad thing, friends, even the things that were not good and maybe even destructive from within that relationship are still able to define us in a positive light if we have learned from them and have come out different/better because of it.

All of this to say, my encouragement to you in this is to not go backwards in life by trying to reclaim the "single you" that once existed, as not only is that impossible—and therefore, will only lead you down the path of destruction for your heart, mind, and life—but it also will never lead to the most mature, authentic, and beautiful you possible. Along these same lines, if and when you are ready to entertain the idea of dating again, keep all of this in mind.

Here's why I say this. As I've already alluded to in this book, we are multi-dimensional creations, which means we have multiple sides that make us who we are. The you that existed with your former spouse can and often does look different than the you in a new relationship. What I mean by this is that we are and can be drawn to very different personalities and types of people in this life based on the varying strong aspects of what makes us who we are. (I would just caution you here to be careful to only lean into the "healthy" aspects/sides of yourself and not the sides that all of us have that tend to allow our "weaknesses/unhealthy" aspects to take center stage.) Instead, what I am referring to is the fact that we are often attracted to people of vastly different passions, skills, and personalities in life because we can have vast differences in these areas too. Therefore, I believe we find that it is our place in life when we enter into a relationship that largely determines which personality and passions in a partner draw us in and speak to us. Because of this, it now makes sense to me that when people remarry after the death of a spouse, their new spouse is often very different from their first. It's because we are different, and that doesn't have to be a bad thing; that is, as long as we are operating from a healthy spirit.

Fifth, I believe it is so important to celebrate each victory along the way, especially in the beginning. No matter how small or trivial they might seem, feel, or look to you, celebrate them! This may look like being able to go an entire day without bursting into tears, or the first time you are able to do more than merely get out of bed, brush your teeth, comb your hair, and eat a meal in a day. These are victories on the road to healing because they require putting one foot in front of the other one day, and then doing it again the next day, and so forth, which means you aren't giving up! As you continue to keep showing up each day in life, you will find that the victories will get bigger and better as the time passes. Who knows, maybe you are like me, and one day, you will find yourself changing out a broken part on your zero turn lawnmower because you can't afford to just buy a new one and your husband had all the necessary tools. So, now you find yourself doing something you never thought possible! Hold on for that day ... it's coming!

Finally, as I was contemplating the last word that I wanted to leave with you, the Lord impressed upon my heart this: Don't ever let other people's opinions, feelings, or the pressures of this world lead you to dismiss or change your story in anyway. As I have heard the saying many times over the years that "Truth doesn't care about your feelings, at the end of the day, it will still be true whether you like it or not." I absolutely believe (because I have experienced this multiple times myself during this journey) that you will have pressure from various sources come your way that will want you to either leave out parts of your story, change it all together, or just don't talk about it, as it is too uncomfortable, not politically correct, or maybe even just too hard for people to deal with emotionally or to hear. It is my firm belief that anyone or anything that would ask you to deny or dismiss any authentic experience you have had is only ever operating from a spirit of self. (Mind you, this is quite often not intentional on the person doing it. Nonetheless, the outcome is the same.) When we operate from under this spirit, we are not able to see, much less honor, the needs of those around us. I have always believed that the truth will always be what's best for people to hear. Therefore, I encourage you to think and live according to the mantra that I have for myself, which is "I will never sacrifice truth on the altar of convenience." This requires knowing who you are at an intimate level. And as you have already read, this comes from intimately knowing whose you are.

My prayer for you, another young widow like me, is that you will allow the Lord God Himself to bind your wounds, strengthen your spirit, give you His peace, which forms the foundation upon which joy, strength, courage, passion, and endurance can exist and thrive, and be the safe place and shelter to which you run. Because when we choose this, oh friends, He promises He will be the father to the fatherless and the husband to the widow. I have seen Him come near to me in my life in both of these intimate ways, and it is for those reasons that I am not only still standing today, but able to move forward with hope and joy into the future of the unknown.

All my love,
Vicki

# Acknowledgments

The list of people who have intentionally walked with me through this time and helped make this book possible is long. I love, respect, and cherish each one of you more than you will ever know!

Paul Green (my cousin). The many selfless and eager ways in which you consistently showed up for me and Tim during the hardest times over the past few years was not only a gift from God to me, but a reminder that the bond and love we share is more than that of just an earthly family. You are one of a kind. Love you, cuz.

Christy Meyer-Vera. You are not only my best friend, but the biological sister I never had. Thank you for truly knowing me and always showing up in the most meaningful ways for what seems like forever. I love you to pieces, Mami!

Dena Ray. Our friendship wouldn't exist without Dave. You are one of the best parts of Dave left with me, and I consider you family. Thank you for being willing to "get in the trenches" and fight/walk through it all with us from the beginning. Our bond goes beyond this side of eternity! Just like Dave, I love you, friend.

Campbell Hy. Watching you evolve from one of my young "mentees" into a loving mentor, source of support, and friend to me over the past few years has been one of the greatest privileges of my life. I am proud and grateful to call you my sweet friend. I couldn't have walked through this time without you. I love you more than you know.

Jamie and Virginia Walden. Even before we knew one another, your words and life's testimony were used to help Dave and I rightly navigate through the confusing days in which we walked. Virginia, the sweet and intimate relationship that you and I have developed over the past few years has been one of mutual support, encouragement, and genuine love. I am incredibly thankful for the "new relationships" the Lord blesses us with at just the right time. Stay the course, and always fight the good fight! I love y'all.

Danny Skolnick and Mindy Lee. Our friendship is a beautiful example of how the Lord works in mysterious ways. It has been nothing short of amazing to watch how the Lord took a "friendly neighbor interaction" and turned it into something intimate and meaningful during what would become the most difficult years of both of our lives. Thank you for always being there in ways that are needed and stepping up when no one else does. Just like Dave did, I love and cherish you both!

Brad and Rachael Powers. Your willingness to persistently seek tangible ways to be there for Dave and me from early on in his illness gave both of us encouragement, strength, and hope when we needed it most. Just as was true for Dave, you will always have a special place in my heart and life. I love y'all.

Gloria Irving. You will probably never know just how much your willingness to immediately jump into action after Dave passed and work tirelessly to help me get the support I needed for the next steps meant and still means to me. You didn't stop there; you have continued loving on me in meaningful ways. Thank you for being a true sister and friend. I love you.

Debbie Christensen. Over the past thirteen years, you have become more than just a next-door neighbor. Your genuine interest in our lives, always-welcoming demeanor, willingness to take care of my chickens and look after my mom during all of the various hospital stays, and presence when I needed a hug or a simple reminder that I was not alone has always been invaluable to me. You are not just a neighbor, but a true friend whom I love.

Amanda DeRiso. You are not just "the mother of Sophie and Simba's best friend," but you have become a friend to me, as well. I cherish the friendship we have developed over the years of living in the same neighborhood, and I absolutely would not have been able to make it these past few years without knowing that I had my dear friend to ensure our dogs had their needs met multiple times and for weeks at a time when I couldn't be home. This has meant more to me than I could ever properly express. I hope you know that I love you!

David Coker. One of the "other Davids"! You were one of Dave's friends with whom he walked much of this life. Your dedication to ensuring that my well-being, safety, and mechanical needs are met now that I am on my own would not only make Dave proud to call you his friend, but eternally grateful. I wouldn't be where I am today without your help. So, thank you!

David Johnson. Another David in my life! I am forever grateful that the Lord brought you into our lives. You were the perfect partner for the film production company, and even more than that, you became a beloved member of our family. Know that as much as you loved and appreciated Dave, he loved and appreciated you. So do I!

Crystal Bovaird. You are more than just the funeral director—who has been a genuine gift from God in my life over the past two-and-a-half years—but you have become a true friend. Never doubt the impact that your thoughtfulness, genuineness, and love that you show families during the most difficult times of their lives matters because it makes all the difference in the world! Love you, friend.

To my team, thank you for partnering with me on this new journey in my life. Your belief, support, and genuine care for this book and me have made it possible for this story to reach the ears of all who need to hear it. Coming to you was definitely a "coming home" experience for me. To my editors and designers, you really are the "unsung heroes" behind this book. Thank you!

# About the Author

Vicki O'Brien is a native Texan with an education and background in medicine, more than twenty-five years of experience as a SAG TV and film actress, and is currently best known for her sought-after expertise and guidance as a professional coach in the world of public speaking with The Moxie Institute. Vicki is known for her relatable style and Southern charm, lifelong passion and work with mentoring teens, as well as her unique ability and desire to connect with others on a deeply personal level. She still calls the Dallas–Fort Worth metroplex home, where she lives on her two-acre homestead.